Alice from Tooting

By Alice Mullen (1879 - 1977)

Including recollections of her daughter
Bertha Mullen (1910 -   )

Edited by Anne Bott

British Library CIP: a catalogue record for this book is available from the British Library

ISBN 0 9516960 4 1

Published 1997 by
PLOWRIGHT PRESS
P O BOX 66
WARWICK CV34 4XE

Orders by direct mail £8.95 (post free UK) or through bookshops

Cover design: 3rd Millenium, Wellesbourne
Printer: Warwick Printing Company Ltd, Warwick

I began this when I was 76, now I'm in
MY Life Story   My 94"

for my dear Bertha

A M Mullen
+ for Sonnie to read as
he will like to know many
things I have written about
Mother

The inscription at the front of Alice's notebook

CONTENTS

Page

EDITOR'S FOREWORD

Alice Mullen wrote her life story in a hard-backed notebook in Biro. On the last page she said it had been done in stages, a little at a time, as is clear from the various references to her age which changes as the notebook progresses. She apparently began it when she was 76 and finished it in her 93rd or 94th year. It is impossible to know which exactly as she gives both - 93rd on the last page and 94th on a front inside cover - and there is no one to ask about the discrepancy.

Bertha Mullen, Alice's daughter, does not know as she had no idea Alice was writing her life story, although it is inscribed twice "for my dear Bertha", and once "and for Lennie (my son) to read".

In Alice's later years Bertha suggested that her mother write an account of her life because she was always fascinated by it and thought it more interesting than many books she had read. She provides details that were left out of the notebook, such as Bertie's death, Christmas, Easter, holidays, household chores, asylum patients.

She says: "The extra information (I have) derives from the many times told accounts from both my Mother and my Grandmother. Grannie lived with us from the time I was a baby till two months before my twentieth birthday. Grannie had the leisure to talk and read to us when Mother was busy with household chores. Many a time I have listened to their reminiscences, as well as the fact that when my aunts came every week to visit Grannie, many of their conversations began with 'Do you remember'?"

My own queries regarding what was in the notebook, Bertha's typing of it and her added memories were answered promptly

i

and with immense patience despite chronic pain and ill health, including a heart attack. Inevitably individuals' memories of events can and do differ and where Alice's and Bertha's recollections diverge to a marked degree this is recorded in a footnote.

In the main Alice's references to her age have been left in. The placing of her memories has also been retained as far as possible, even if this rather throws out the chronology (for example, the recollections of her schooling on page 28), as the context for the raising of those memories is interesting. Curved brackets in the text were used by Alice or represent additions by Bertha; square brackets indicate an addition by the editor.

Clarification is needed of the use of the word 'lady'; two meanings at least are apparent in the text. One indicates a woman with more money, a middle-class rather than a working-class woman, for example Alice's dressmaking customers. The other is a polite way of referring to women, such as the reference to ladies being daring if they smoked (page 90). A further explanation of what Alice meant in general by 'lady' is given by Bertha.

"'Ladies' refers more to the manner and character of a person than the money they had, the clothes they wore, or their social status. Mother and her sisters would have been at home in any company. They had moneyed and talented friends - one was a member of the Royal Academy, two were surgeons, another a Greek scholar. They were never ashamed of being poor; they would have been ashamed of being rude or dishonest, or untrustworthy, or patronising."

Alice and her sisters were ambitious and wanted to get on, but had few options for doing so. Bertha says their going into service was a preliminary to better things. For Alice and Ruth this was nursing, while Aggie and Nellie went into children's work.

Apart from being ambitious, Alice was, according to her daughter: "quiet, serious, but with a great sense of humour. She was very patient, practical, but also poetical. She had a lively mind and a good memory. As she got older she became more introspective, a bit secretive. She liked to keep control of the housekeeping, and only relinquished the reins with a great deal of persuasion.

"She was always ladylike and neat in appearance. She was very observant and good at summing up characters. She made many friends and kept them till they died. She was sociable - belonging to several groups at chapel when she lived near enough - a good listener, and trustworthy. She did not repeat gossip."

My thanks to the many friendly and extremely helpful staff at record offices and libraries - Bournemouth Library, Brighton Reference Library, Essex Record Office, Greater London Record Office, Hertford Local History Library, Hertford Record Office, Mitcham Reference Library, Morden Reference Library, National Army Museum, Norfolk Record Office, Norfolk Studies, Redditch Family History Centre, Royal Archives at Windsor Castle, Tony Shaw at Wandsworth Local History Library, and the Wellcome Institute for the History of Medicine especially Sue Gold. And thanks to Irene Yates for suggesting to Bertha that Plowright Press might be interested in her mother's notebook.

Anne Bott
Warwick, 1996

I was sent with a message to the Dr only to be told by his wife he would come later on as he had to rest I think through a slight accident he used to ride about in a dogcart it was a light high vehicle , when I got back the midwife said you go back, & tell the Dr your mother will die if he does not come, I ran as I had never run in my life, I felt I would never stop, the doctors wife got that message as I had it, & soon came, we all had to go to a neighbours to dinner, & the others went back to School, I stayed in the neighbours & could hear the two sisters in law talking quietly & seriously over the garden fence & I thought it was about my mother, later on they told me we had a baby brother, he was born on his fathers birthday the midwife used to come each day & I slept with mother, one night we heard our down stair window open it went down with a bang & all was quiet the sash of the window were broken & the burglar went off, but got in a few doors away

A sample page of Alice's notebook

ALICE'S FAMILY TREE

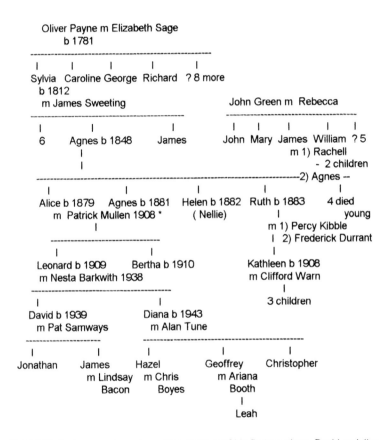

```
Oliver Payne m Elizabeth Sage
        b 1781
-----------------------------------------------
   |        |        |        |         |
 Sylvia  Caroline George  Richard   ? 8 more
 b 1812
 m James Sweeting                    John Green m  Rebecca
------------------------------------       ------------------------------------
   |        |              |          |      |      |        |        |
   6     Agnes b 1848    James      John   Mary   James   William  ? 5
              |                                    m 1) Rachell
              |                                      - 2 children
-----------------------------------------------------------2) Agnes --
   |              |              |              |              |
 Alice b 1879  Agnes b 1881  Helen b 1882  Ruth b 1883    4 died
   m  Patrick Mullen 1908 *  ( Nellie)        |            young
        |                               m 1) Percy Kibble
  ----------------------------------    | 2) Frederick Durrant
        |              |                      |
 Leonard b 1909    Bertha b 1910     Kathleen b 1908
 m Nesta Barkwith 1938               m Clifford Warn
 ---------------------------------------        |
   |                     |                  3 children
 David b 1939        Diana b 1943
 m Pat Samways       m Alan Tune
 ----------------------  -----------------------------------------------
   |        |        |              |              |
Jonathan  James   Hazel        Geoffrey      Christopher
         m Lindsay m Chris      m Ariana
         Bacon    Boyes         Booth
                                  |
                                 Leah
```

* This was Patrick Mullen's second marriage. Two children of his first marriage, David and Jim, were alive when he married Alice.

1

1. BEGINNINGS IN MERTON

I arrived suddenly, head first into the midwife's linen apron, on 11 December 1879.

Mother had two attempts to produce a child before me. The first baby was stillborn, but soon she became pregnant again. She had a protracted labour and finally a doctor was called. He consulted another and they decided that my mother was too small to have a natural birth. They made the decision to cut the baby up inside the womb and remove it piecemeal.[1]

My mother suffered agonies.[2] They called in a neighbour to clean up and Mother used to tell that her bedroom was like a butcher's shop. She had a horror of calling in a doctor for years and that is probably why some of her confinements were not what they should have been. She was told not to go to full term again, but dreaded further surgical interference.

The little house where I was born was in High Street, Merton, Surrey, now part of south London. On the day of my birth a man called round with a cart full of potatoes about 4 o'clock in the afternoon. My parents moved to the house in late autumn and were unable to plant vegetables. Mother bought a 56 lb [25.5 kg] sack of potatoes from him and he dumped them just inside the front door.

After he had gone, she thought it would not do to leave them there in case my father came home from work and fell over the sack in the dark. There was no light in the passage.

---

[1] This was not uncommon. Caesarean section in Britain was still considered so dangerous that it was the last resort, performed rarely on living women. - Editor.
[2] She may have been given some laudanum, or chloroform. - Bertha Mullen.

2

She tried to drag the sack to the kitchen.

Suddenly she felt a strong pain. She got to the front door and called a child and sent her for the neighbour who had agreed to act as midwife. Slowly she managed to get upstairs to the bedroom. The fire was laid in the grate and she stooped to light it.

Just then the midwife arrived. As she raised my mother up I hurtled into the world. For years after, whenever she chanced to meet me, she would say: "Ah you are the young lady who could not wait to be born in bed like anyone else. Are you still in such a hurry?" I was named Alice Mary, the second name being after my favourite aunt.[3]

---

[3] I think she was named Alice after one of the sisters of Mrs Hampton (former employer). This prompted Mrs Hampton to tell Alice she was sorry no girl had been named after her. Alice said if she had a daughter she would be named Bertha after Mrs Hampton. BM.

2. MOTHER WAS FROM HERTFORDSHIRE

Both my parents were from the country, Mother from Bedmond in Hertfordshire, and Father from Wortwell in Norfolk. My mother's grandmother Elizabeth Sage was granddaughter of the Baron Saye and Sele. She married Oliver Payne, shoemaker, at Abbots Langley Parish Church and they had about 12 children. I still have a photo of her in a black silk dress and a cap or bonnet with goffered frill round her face [see next page].

She was a godly woman and did not want to be a trouble to anyone, particularly as she got older. She was concerned that she might need care and become a burden.

One night she called out to her son, Richard. He went into her room and saw her sitting on the side of the bed. She said: "Kiss me, Richard. I'm about to witness a great change. I've seen my husband and my saviour." He kissed her and she fell back on the bed, dead.

Her mother in law lived to be 108 and opened a ball at Langley House, Abbots Langley, in her 108th year.

Her daughter Sylvia was born in 1812. Sylvia was my grandmother. She married James Sweeting, son of shoemaker Edward Sweeting of Ganders Ash, a hamlet in the parish of Watford, and my mother, Agnes Selina, was their seventh child, born in 1848.

Sylvia had a sharp tongue. Her husband left her and she took Mother and went back to the family home where, at the time of the 1851 Census, she was working as a needlewoman, work that two unmarried sisters, Diannah and Ann, were doing also. Later he returned and Mother's brother Jim was born but he soon left again.

4

Elizabeth Sage: Alice's great-grandmother

3. FATHER WAS A NORFOLK MAN

My father, James, was the second son of John Green, of Wortwell, Norfolk, master shoemaker, village postmaster and latterly farmer of 11 acres. He was the Census enumerator and was well respected, the 'squire' of the village.

Father had at least three brothers and four sisters, one, Rosa, a school mistress, and another, Mary, companion to a lady in the west London area. He married and had two children but his first wife died.

He did all sorts of work, gardening, carpentry, labouring, and he found work as a gardener at Wimbledon, which was where my mother met him. She was a cook for Colonel and Mrs Hampton near by.

She fell in love with his big hazel eyes and dark curly hair, and was entranced by his velvet coat and embroidered waistcoat and his ability to ride a penny farthing bicycle which he used to do when he came courting.

In time my mother got to know his sister Mary, a truly Christian woman. We all loved her, she was so sweet and understanding. She died of breast cancer in her fifties.

4. WEDDING IN WIMBLEDON

My parents were married on Christmas Eve, 1876, at Wimbledon Parish Church. My mother's wedding gown was a silk dress which stood up by itself. An Indian shawl was a present from the colonel's wife and a muff from his daughters. She wore a straw bonnet with velvet ribbons and a bunch of cherries.

Afterwards my parents walked to their new lodgings. Two rooms had been taken with a respectable couple near by and the landlady had promised to cook them a nice roast dinner. However, when they knocked it was the husband who answered the door in a very flustered state. He was in his shirt sleeves and wore, tied round his middle, one of his wife's aprons. There was no smell of cooking.

The young husband said his wife had gone into premature labour and the neighbours were unwilling to leave their families at such a time to help. He did not know what to do as this was the first baby and he knew nothing of confinements.

My mother told the husband to heat some water, then went to her bedroom and opened her box. She put on a serge dress of dark grey, tied on a large white apron and went to the young wife. A trained midwife or doctor were unthought of, except in a case of extremity, where people were poor.

All day the labour went on. My mother tied two cords to the foot of the bed for the young woman to pull on. From time to time she went downstairs. The husband and James had a meal of bread and cheese and beer, while my mother made tea and cut bread and butter for herself and the wife.

It was late in the evening when the baby appeared and both his mother and my mother were exhausted. When the new mother and her son were washed and made comfortable, my mother gathered up the pile of soiled clothing and bed linen and carried it downstairs. The fire was out and in the large Windsor chairs sprawled James and the new father, fast asleep. She woke them and sent them upstairs to bed.

Then she went into the washhouse, filled the copper [boiler] and lit the fire under it. She had to fetch the water from the rain water barrel outside the back door, to fill both the copper and the washtub. It was very cold and she was glad of the warmth from the copper.

The church clock struck midnight as she finished washing the last of the linen. She opened the back door to greet the Christmas morning and found it was snowing heavily.

Dipping up hot water from the copper, she took a bucket and brush and began to clean the flags. She tipped away the dirty water and became aware of the silence. Even the snow slipped into place silently. She suddenly felt quite alone.

What a wedding day! What a wedding night! She took off her apron and put it to soak before going upstairs to creep into bed beside her husband. He did not wake but snored all night.

This was the story of her wedding day that my mother used to tell us. Invariably we said: "But did she really want the baby for Christmas? Couldn't she have waited? Perhaps she didn't have anything else for her husband's Christmas present."

There were plenty of houses to rent, and they found a cottage in Merton. This was before they went to the house in High Street.

The first thing I remember must have happened when I was 18 months old, as my sister Agnes was born in the March 1881 when I was 15 months. I remember my mother taking the baby in long clothes in her arms, and me by the hand, to a house with two steps at the front door, then leaving me with some people and going away with the baby.

I know I screamed at the door, and it's the only time I can remember screaming, as I thought she had gone for good. I don't know how long I was left, but years after I told Mother I remembered this and she said: "Oh yes I had to leave you with Mrs Wilkes, as I couldn't manage to carry two babies." She had some distance to go and had no pram at this time.

The next March my sister Nellie (Helen) was born, and in August 1883 my sister Ruth.

One afternoon Mother went upstairs to fetch the babies down from their nap and I heard her say she wanted a knife, so I fetched one from the kitchen and was just about to climb the stairs when she threw down a pillow to put in the pram. She had a baby under each arm and could not manage the pillow as well.

It caught the knife, which cut my upper lip. Mother was coming down the stairs when she heard me cry out and she nearly fell when she saw the blood. I still carry the scar.

The next baby arrived in 1884. Mother asked me to choose her name. I could not think, so a flower name, very popular then, was suggested. My idea was Wallflower. Finally I became resigned to Violet, but a neighbour who had been very kind wanted her to be Harriet, so she was Harriet Violet, but we called her Violet as she

9

had big purple eyes. Poor Mother had three babies to do for, my sister Nellie being weak, and two little ones running about.

One Saturday morning about four months later she washed the babies and put them to sleep, two in the big cradle and the young baby in her bed.

Mother was busy all the morning and when she went up to fetch the two babies down my father came home and called to say he wanted his dinner quickly as he had to go out. Mother hurried down to attend to him, not looking into her bedroom at the baby who was quiet.

After Father had finished his dinner and had gone out, she went up for the baby, to find she had turned over on her face and become twisted in her long nightgown and was in convulsions. She did all she could to save her but the lovely baby died.

She was put in a little coffin on a chest of drawers. I remember getting a chair and standing on it to see what had happened to the dear baby. I saw two pennies placed on her eyes. These I took off thinking she would wake up. It was very sad and I remember the inquest because there was a soldier in red uniform.

Our neighbours next door were a childless couple named Pitt. They were very fond of my sister Agnes. She was quite independent and would get her own way. They nicknamed her Tommy (tomboy), and Tommy she was for years. I've been told that when she was born and I was taken up to see her, my exclamation was: "Dear ickle sing, bless her ickle heart!" and I tried to care for her by rocking her cradle and singing to her.

When she was nearly five my cousin Mary came and took her back for a visit to London. My cousin was an only child and grown up but she was fond of children and did all she could to give Aggie a good time.

10

I well remember her coming home perhaps a week or fortnight after, and how I was looking forward to it. But as soon as she was home she was down the garden path and into Mrs Pitt's next door, with all her exciting news. She stayed to tea and when she came back it was bed time. I was sure she would talk to me in bed but she just went to sleep and I was so disappointed.

Overleaf: *Tooting, 1888. The fever hospitals, Fountain Hospital and Grove Hospital, were built next to each other in the open area bounded on two sides by Fountain Road and Blackshaw Road. Map courtesy of Wandsworth Local History Library*

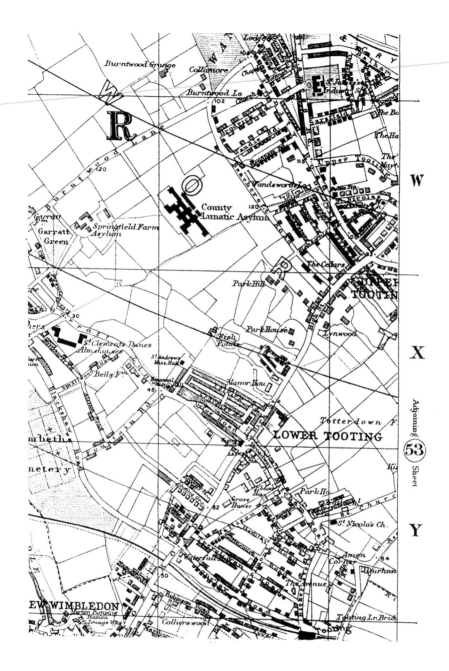

6. STARTING SCHOOL

Soon after this we were taken to school and I remember it so well. There was a big iron stove in one corner of the room. We all sat on backless benches and the bigger girls (but not the boys) had to sit with books on their heads to aid deportment, unless sewing or writing.

We were given slates to write on, and of course just scribbled as we could not write. When the teacher came round she picked up our slates and in a loud voice said: "Rubbish, rubbish." I did not know what rubbish was, but I knew by her tone she disdained our efforts. She then set us to make pot hooks and hangers.

I do not remember anything else about that school apart from the big girl who took us and brought us home, and who one day wanted to go across the fields towards the river Wandle to get forgetmenots. I would not budge, as I had a fear of that river, having escaped drowning in it when about three years old and I can still remember those dark swiftly running waters now as I rolled over so near and my muff went in while Mother caught me by my little coat and frock.

It was a cold windy day and Mother was wheeling the pram with the two younger babies and I was trotting along behind her when I lost my footing. There was no wall over the bridge, only posts and chains. I heard the men in a trap call out: "She's in, she's in."

But mercifully I was saved that terrible end, though I heard a few years later of another neighbour's little girl who did fall in at the same place and was carried a long way and her body not found for weeks. I believe that was the oldest and narrowest bridge in England.

There were several mills working at that time, the flour mills, and the copper mills, we were used to the continual noise from the copper mills, the textile mills, the other mill was the paper mill and may be yet. At one time Nelson lived near here, and I've seen the last of Merton Abbey. Just a little sunken gateway was still there in 1914.

7. MOVE TO LOWER TOOTING

When I was six we moved to Lower Tooting. It was a terrace house facing an open space we called the green, and strange to say our neighbours on the right were another childless couple.

The man worked at the dye works and was quite yellow, his wife was hunch back. They were both under 5 ft [1.52 m] and took notice of my sister Agnes. She may have made the advances and I expect she did. Soon she was their Tommy and on Saturday she would go in to them for dinner.

Mother took us to our new school, and we went by an enclosed field. It was an oval and called the parson's field, there were some cottages one side and the parsonage.

Mother thought I would be able to find my way home but I evidently went the other side of the field and could not recognise anything apart from the palings, so I soon began to cry thinking we were lost, when a motherly woman asked me where I came from.

I said our "new house", then another woman said: "Oh I expect it's the people who moved into Hazelhurst," so she took us to the end of our road and pointed out the other side of the field. After that I knew there were two ways and I would not be lost whichever way I might come home.

Poor Mother had another baby in that house who we named Christine Elizabeth. She only lived a few months and I stood by Mother as she held the dear baby on her lap one evening and saw her die.

15

Mother was in poor health and the baby suffered. The babies came so fast and were not strong and in those days there were no clinics or even milk for mothers with a lot of young children.

Father grew vegetables and Mother looked after hens when she could afford them and we had to exist on vegetables and a few eggs. She also kept a pig when she could but the meat generally had to be sold.

The pig had a sty at the bottom of the garden and was invariably called Betsy. Mother used to take a bath of soapsuds after she had done the washing and a hard broom and give Betsy a scrub, but we children were not allowed in the sty.

8. FROCK CAUGHT FIRE

We all had to go to school, even my youngest sister at that time, Ruth, she was four and I had to look after her and my other sisters. Mother was working, she helped at a cottage laundry doing fine ironing and the mending, and when I came home at dinner time I had to put the potatoes on and sometimes the fire would be quite out. They were old open grates with two hobs and an oven.

One day I got the sticks of firewood which were long and lit the fire up, and in turning round my frock and petticoats at the back caught fire. I only knew when my little sisters got on the chairs and screamed, but Aggie or Tommy as she was called, rushed out of the house to meet Mother and tell her.

But I had rolled myself in the hearthrug over and over, because I remembered my mother reading to us from one of our little Sunday school library books of a man rolling a child in a rug to put out the fire.

So once again I was wonderfully preserved. I look back and see God's love in all my life's experiences.

9. SUNDAY SCHOOL

Mother used to take us up to bed and teach us to say our prayers, and I was about four or five when I began to understand the greatness and wonder of God. I remember one night going to the back door and looking up at the sky and thinking God is up there, how wonderful, above the stars.

Often as a child I looked up and as time went on, life was hard and I longed to be there. Mother was so often tried and her patience gave out. She was very quick tempered and there was the stick very quickly or anything else handy. I generally got the blame for anything that went wrong.

I loved my Sunday school and every moment spent there. My teacher was kind and there were no harsh words. I had very little schooling as being the eldest, there were babies to care for, and Mother had to work, so that fell to me and I loved the babies. But when I was attending Sunday school I would carry the baby with me rather than miss Sunday school.

We used to get a motto, or large text, if we learnt our verses. One I had I remember so well was 'Blessed is the man whose transgression is forgiven, whose sin is covered'. I used to read it as it hung on the bedroom wall, and think it would be a wonderful thing to be blessed like that. I was about 10 then, and anything I did wrong troubled me.

I used to ask God to forgive me and wash me from sin, and please take me to heaven then I wouldn't do anything else wrong or sin.

I could not understand, how it was, and could not talk to anyone. One Sunday we had a gentleman address the Sunday school and at the end he asked any children who wanted to be the Lord's to

18

stay. I stayed, but Aggie took the others home, and whatever was said to us I can never remember, because I got into such trouble as soon as I entered the house, my sister having told Mother I would not come home.

Alice's Mother, Agnes Selina

10. BROTHER BERTIE IS BORN

My little brother was born in the November before my 10th birthday in the December, and my father was away at Margate working. He had said the work would last and we had better move down there, so our things were mostly packed, then he wrote to say the winds were very strong and he did not think I could stand them as I used to suffer with bronchitis every winter.

Keeping two homes was the trouble and splitting the money, it was not much he could send after paying for his board. Then Mother heard of an elderly retired man who wanted to have an house with a field at the back like ours to keep poultry. It was arranged for him to have the house, but we had to stay until after the baby arrived.

It was a very bad time for Mother, although she longed for a son. The midwife came and stayed. I was kept home from school and was sent with a message to the doctor, only to be told by his wife he would come later on as he had to rest, I think through a slight accident, a fall. He used to ride about in a dogcart, it was a light high vehicle.

When I got back the midwife said you go back and tell the doctor your mother will die if he does not come. I ran as I had never run in my life, I felt I would never stop.

The doctor's wife got that message as I had it, and he soon came. We all had to go to a neighbour's to dinner, and the others went back to school. I stayed in the neighbour's and could hear the two sisters in law talking quietly and seriously over the garden fence and I thought it was about my mother.

Later on they told me we had a baby brother, he was born on his father's birthday. Mother named him Gilbert (Bertie), and he was her darling always.

The midwife used to come each day and I slept with Mother. One night we heard our downstairs window open, it went down with a bang and all was quiet. Mother lit the candle and called out before going downstairs, with me creeping behind her. The sash window in the front room was right down.

A burglar had prised the window open, when the sash cords broke and he went off, but got in a few doors away and took the man's overcoat and several other things.

11. TOOTING GROVE

Mr Templeman who wanted our house came and asked if he could have possession of the downstairs front room and kitchen. We managed with the bedrooms and scullery.

He was a strange old man. He was gaunt, with a straggly beard and grizzled head, and he wore leather leggings. He kept a gun in his room and refused entry to visitors. He built an enormous shed in the garden and had lots of poultry sent to put in it. Gone was our freedom and enjoyment of the house and garden, for he took over and objected to any noise.

Mother was most uncomfortable for it was so inconvenient. She was glad to find a very small cottage not far away to move into.

It had a front room you entered from the street, no hall, a room for a kitchen beyond and then a scullery, with a long low stone sink, no tap water, but a spring running into a stone trough in the garden and all our water had to be fetched in a bucket. It was lovely water always running. Three houses used this spring, but we had our own earth closet with a scrubbed box for a seat in which there were two holes of different sizes.

There was a field beyond the garden with a low fence. It was easy to get into the field in the summer, but we did not stay there long.

There were some winding little stairs up to a big bedroom running right across without partition. It was cold, and Mother hung a curtain across halfway. When Father came home he did not like it. He got work nearer home, and we moved to a terrace house in what was called Tooting Grove.

I used to mind the baby and carry him about as we had no pram, and when he was about seven or eight months old Mother was ill with a miscarriage. We had only just settled into that house.

Jung's the baker's on the left, at the corner of Defoe Road and Tooting High Street, looking northwards from the Broadway towards Balham. c 1890's. Picture courtesy of Wandsworth Local History Library

23

12. AUNT CAROLINE'S IN CHEAPSIDE

When I was 11 my mother's older sister Caroline came to see us, she lived in Queen Street, Cheapside, in London. She proposed to take one of us girls for a while to relieve Mother, as her daughter, my cousin Mary, was married and abroad.

My parents decided I was to go as I had begun fainting and Mother thought I would get more food and get stronger. A carpetbag was packed with my clothes, my little Bible and a book which had been a Sunday school prize, and the next week Mother took me up.

Uncle Bailey had been a soldier and they had been abroad. When he was pensioned from the army, Aunt Caroline did not wish to live in the country, so she persuaded him to get a place in the City. They were caretakers for offices, there were several floors occupied by solicitors, and my aunt and uncle had a flat at the top of the premises with a little roof garden on the leads.

My uncle had a large beard and was quiet and soldierly. My aunt was plumper and sharp tongued, outspoken and critical, decidedly the dominant one.

The next morning my uncle took me to a doctor and I was surprised to be asked to undress and to have my chest sounded with a stethoscope. He ordered cod liver oil, plenty of good food and fresh air. It seemed strange to have to go to the heart of London to get it. I could have taken the cod liver oil if only they had given me something to drink after each dose. Every time I took it I felt sick, I used to dread it.

I was given good food but my aunt insisted on my eating lumps of fat and gristle. With the greatest difficulty I used to hide these in my handkerchief and wait for the opportunity to put them down the toilet. Then I had the horror of fearing that I might have stopped the drains. It was considered a sin to leave anything on your plate.

While with my aunt she sent me with a note to the barber where my uncle used to go, and I got a shock when he put a sheet round me and cut off all my hair, making me look like a boy.

We all had long hair, all girls did in those days, it was only cut when they had ringworm or were suffering from a severe fever, but my aunt said when I went back she couldn't be bothered doing hair. I could have managed it myself. I know the other children used to say: "That girl looks like a boy." I did hope it would grow quickly.

My aunt did not send me to school, I had to help her do the offices. I was used to work and did not think anything about that. My job was to dust, and very dusty, musty smelling places they were. The brown walls, dark green linoleum and green shades at the windows no doubt created an impression of gloom, as well as the piles of papers tied with red tape, the box files and tin deed boxes. There were also three flights of stairs to be cleaned.

After the work was done my aunt would sometimes take me to St Paul's Cathedral and we sat outside in the sun and she did her tatting.

13. SCHOOLING IS OVER

My aunt sent me to a Sunday school when she wanted an afternoon's quiet and some of the children asked me where I went to school. When I said I did not go anywhere, they said I should be sure to get into trouble from the School Board. When I told my aunt she said: "You can say your uncle is teaching you."

The next day she bought three copy books and I had to sit and copy the proverbs they contained and show them to my uncle. That was all the instruction I received.

So my schooling was over, I never went to school again. But Father and Mother taught me, and I picked up all I could from my sisters, who brought work home which I copied, and from books as well as the newspaper. Later on I taught myself some Latin to help with the nursing and dispensing.

My uncle used to sit out on the leads to read his paper and I was allowed to read it when it was finished with, and I liked it there. That part of London was very quiet at night and of a Sunday. He grew flowers in boxes, and some beans, and had a honeysuckle which smelt very sweet. But I missed my home, and the company of my sisters and little brother.

After about six months Mother wrote to her sister and asked her to come for a visit. Aunt was so cross about it. It seems Mother had said our peas and new potatoes were nice and could we come to dinner. I could not understand why she was so cross and said she could buy peas and potatoes herself.

She answered Mother's letter and whatever she said, it ended with Mother coming for me, and taking me back home.

When we reached Tooting we called at the nursery for my little brother, who had been taken there each day while Mother was at work. I was so looking forward to seeing him, but poor little baby he did not know me, and would not come to me, even my sisters thought me strange and no wonder, with my short hair.

Alice aged 17

14. IN TROUBLE

Tooting was only a small place at that time and the fields round about were our joy. Where they eventually built two fever hospitals,[4] when the village began to grow, were lovely fields and big trees, little streams running clear along one field and another coming out by the side of the road, and above it a lovely hawthorn hedge and some big white convolvulus grew there. We used to call them white lilies. There were several springs with water always running, one near the church.

While we lived in the house where my little brother was born, we used to have to walk nearly two miles to school, and sometimes our boots and stockings would be wet through as there were no proper paths for us. We sometimes climbed along the fences to keep out of big puddles, and the teacher would come in and ask about the little Greens, and we would have to sit round the fire while our boots and stockings dried.

When there was room my sisters were told they were to go to Tooting Graveney school, that was much nearer.

We all wore holland pinafores. They were hard wearing and stood up to a good deal of washing, and they were worn summer and winter. We also wore blue ones with white spots I remember, but they were more delicate.

We had to pay so much a week, even a few pennies, and there were no mid morning drinks. Once I lost the school money and had to retrace my steps until I found where I had dropped it in the long grass, still tied up in my handkerchief.

---

[4] Fountain and Grove hospitals, Tooting Grove, were built next to each other in the 1890s. - Editor.

28

One day I had to take my father his dinner and crossing a field I kicked against what I at first thought were eggshells, but they were soft and I took them home to Mother. She said they were mushrooms, and they grew in the night. I told my sisters when we went to bed and we thought it would be a lovely idea to get up early without waking Mother and get some more.

We managed by going down in our stockings and we must have been very quiet. I took them to the field and of course the grass was very wet with heavy dew. We got a few mushrooms, but our boots and stockings were very wet and we had no others.

One tea time when we came home from school our boots were all wet. I made up the fire, as Mother had gone to nurse a sick neighbour, and gave the others their tea and promised if they were good to have a nice game before we went to bed, and to be fair put one of each pair of boots nearer the fire to dry.

This particular evening we all went to bed when it was dusk. Next morning our boots were hard, especially the ones that had been too near the fire. Poor Mother and poor me, for I was punished. So often I did things for the best and then they turned out to be wrong. I was so young and tried to manage but had not enough judgment about some things.

Another evening I thought if I made everything nice and made up the fire and put the kettle near to be ready for Mother, we could all go and meet her up the fields. It was the only tin kettle we had, from a passing tinker, our other kettles were iron. I shut the door and gave my sister Nellie the key because she had a coat with a pocket in it.

We walked up and down and it was such a long time before Mother came, she used to have to work long hours. When we got home she said: "Where is the key?" I said:"Nellie has it," but Nellie said she hadn't, and as it could not be found Mother got the boy next door to climb through the kitchen window. When we got in the kettle had boiled dry and had a hole in the bottom, and the fire was down.

Long after the key was found in the hem of Nellie's coat, but I got into trouble, over these accidents. I was under 10 when these things happened.

My sister Ruth and I inherited Father's dark curly hair and hazel eyes. Aggie and Nellie had long straight brown hair like Mother and blue eyes. Once I felt sorry for Nellie and tied her hair up in tight rags at night, hoping it would be curly by morning. When the rags were removed it fuzzed out and when Mother saw it she said I was trying to make the poor child look like a Hottentot, and called for a basin of water and a hairbrush to smooth it down again.

Nellie cooked the pudding one day when I was ill with rheumatic fever. It was a suet roly poly and she brought me up a slice. When I asked if there was not even a pinch of brown sugar to go with it, she said: "It's a currant pudding. I put in one for each of you and none for myself, as I don't like currants."

Another thing I remember, it was Queen Victoria's Jubilee 1887, and I was away from school through illness and so lost my mug. I often had to miss things such as Sunday school treats, but once Mother took me to the station just in time to join the others going to Ashtead Woods. It was such a surprise as I had no expectation of going.

She gave me two pennies [less than 1p] and told me to spend them on a glass of milk and a bar of chocolate, and I was not to run races or try to skip. The other children had money to spend and they won prizes for running and jumping and skipping but I did as Mother had told me and had a very nice day.

15. MONKEY PUZZLE

Once I went to my Sunday school teacher's house for the afternoon and tea. All our class were invited. We had all been given six packets of flower seeds in the spring and were to bring a bunch of flowers from them to be judged by her father who took a great interest in gardening and grew rare flowers and shrubs.

I did want to go to this but had no light dress like the other children. There was a white dress with little sprigs in mauve and black, it was too big for me. We sometimes had some of my cousin's things, they were too big as she was older, but I got this dress of Mary's and put tucks in it to shorten it, as I knew Mother would not have time.

I went with my bunch of flowers. We had a lovely time in the garden and we had our photos taken in a group, the first time I had ever had a photo. I won the prize for my bunch of flowers.

As our teacher's father studied phrenology he felt the bumps of our heads and I could not remember all he said, but one was a good bump for construction, which was very true, but by the time I reached home with my big pot of white chrysanthemum as prize, I had got it all mixed up.

After telling them some of my bumps I ended up with a big bump of destruction. Of course they laughed at me and I got some teasing.

One other instance I remember when I was about eight a sample of Monkey brand soap was put through the letter box. I read it was soap and won't wash clothes, so I thought it must be to wash people. I did not realize it was an abrasive, and I told the others I would wash them with the new soap. I did, and we all had shining faces, though I don't think we suffered from the mistake.

31

My father seldom took a great deal of notice of us, but he did remember my seventh birthday and bought me a pink and white china mug, which was fluted and had gilt edges. I kept that mug for 40 years.

It had some little sweets inside, but I had toothache and I could not eat them, and my sister Ruth thought if I could not, she would, and climbed up to the shelf and ran off with them, and ate the lot. Another time Father took me with him when he visited his sister Mary, and bought me a glass of milk and a bun at a dairy.

One day Mother bought a pomegranate and divided it between us. I thought it a wonderful thing and we called it a 'jewel fruit'. We never saw tomatoes for years and when we did they were light in colour, not like the lovely home grown ones we have now. Some people called them 'love apples' but then there was a scare because someone put it about that they gave people cancer, so they did not become popular for some time.

We never saw bananas till I was grown, but we had plenty of apples and sometimes a few oranges.

16. UNCLE JIM VISITS

Sometimes my mother's youngest brother would come to see us and stay a night. We all loved Uncle Jim, he would tell us stories and sing to us. He brought a Gladstone bag full of things, russet apples, pears, nuts and little presents for each of the children, as well as something for Mother. Sometimes I believe it was money because he could see the state of things. She loved new green peas and he always brought her some on her birthday, 6 October.

He was married to the school mistress at the village school at Bedmond. They lived in a cottage with Tudor chimneys and a stair leading out of the parlour to an underground room under the next house where Aunt Annie kept all her preserves. There was also a secret room upstairs leading out of a cupboard in their panelled bedroom.

The garden was beautiful and besides the ordinary well there was a square well about 3-4 ft deep, bricked round and lined with ferns. It was a cold store in which milk, butter and meat were kept. My uncle loved children, although he was childless, and let us clamber on his knees, something Father did not permit. My uncle was always so pleasant and placid.

Once he brought some old books and oh they were treasures. My sister Nellie had one called The Dolls' Wash [by Juliana Horatia Ewing]. We went through that book till we knew it by heart. The little girls washed their dolls' clothes, and one said after the washing was done:

> I'm glad we did it you know,
> But I'm gladder still that it's done,
> And Victoria's dress will never come white,
> Because it was used for a duster.

33

I claimed a little book with quaint pictures and read it through, it was Bunyan's Pilgrim's Progress. I read it again and again, and could still repeat some of the opening chapters though I'm now 76.

Mother, Alice (standing) and Nellie. Part of a photo of the four sisters and Mother, about 1897. The photo was later torn

17. SUNDAY READING

No unnecessary work was done on Sunday and Mother would read to us some Sunday evenings, new books were often kept for Sunday. The day was mostly kept for singing hymns and reading Scriptures but drawing and painting were allowed.

Both Mother and Father loved Shakespeare and always had books in the house. They were well read in history and the Bible.

Mother encouraged us to read at an early age. We were brought up on the classics and Dickens as well as Shakespeare, but she did not neglect Jane Austen or the Brontes.

We were never allowed to read poorly written material. She abhorred comic papers when they came in. But we read the newspaper when Father had finished with it. It was then cut into squares and used in the toilet.

Father used to hear us say our tables and make us calculate how many seed potatoes he would need to sow such or such an area of ground.

18. THE RAG BAG

I used to dress my sisters and myself up in various things. Mother used to go over to Wimbledon from time to time to visit the Hamptons, and in a bag they used to put clothes they had finished with, and pieces of material from dresses and garments they had had made, and call it the rag bag, and give it to Mother knowing she would make use of everything.

We thought it lovely to see and turn out these things and guess which would end up as clothes for us.

When I first went to school with my sister Agnes, Mother had gone to Wimbledon and had left my sister Nellie with a neighbour but she cried so and they could not pacify her, so when we came home from school they called me in, and they thought it very strange because I said: "Don't cry duckie and you shall look in the rag bag."

It acted like magic. They told Mother, and I expect she explained, but it was always a saying at home: "Don't cry duckie and you shall look in the rag bag."

There were some bustles made of some wire and stiff material that ladies used to wear at the back under the skirts. We thought it great fun to put these on.

At one time three of us used to sleep together in a big wooden bed. We were sent to bed early and light evenings we used to sit up and choose from the patchwork quilt which pieces of cotton or velvet we would like dresses made of, or bonnets trimmed with silk.

This bed had wooden lathes and I expect the wood must have been worm eaten and after moving to another house the bed was

36

put up and we were put to bed but in the night there was a mighty crack and we all went down with the bedding, leaving the framework and posts. My mother told us to stay there as there was nothing she could do. We did not mind as it seemed an adventure to be bundled up together with the mattress on the floor.

For a little while she put some boxes under the mattress and we had to sleep like that until she could afford to get another second hand bed.

Out of our bedroom there was another little bedroom down three stairs. When it was wet in our holidays we played in this room. We had no toys apart from a piece of rope for skipping and a penny peg top, and the games I used to think of were acting Bible stories, or Shakespeare. One day we decided to play Joseph in the pit. Nellie, being the smallest and lightest, had to be Joseph.

I found the dirty sheets ready for the wash and Aggie and I held two corners while Ruth stood below and braced herself against the cradle which was the pit. We swung Nellie down but there was an awful splitting sound and the sheet tore in two and Nellie slipped through into the cradle. She was not hurt and we put the cradle back and I took the sheet downstairs, knowing I should have to tell Mother.

At dinner time Mother came in, tired and upset about something at the laundry, and Aggie had to tell her first and assure her it was all my idea. She seized the nearest thing, a child's boot, and swung it and cut my head open. Putting a pad and bandage on, she said: "Let this be a lesson to you in future," and went on cooking the dinner.

We had to mend the sheet by turning sides to middle, putting the worn middle parts on the outside while the two outsides were joined in the middle. Then the rough edges were hemmed.

19. CATS' TEETH WILL NEVER DO

Mother taught us all to sew by the time we were four. We had to make neat stitches. If we made large ones, she would unpick our work, saying: "Cats' teeth. Cats' teeth will never do."

We progressed to simple embroidery stitches, especially featherstitching which was used on ladies' underwear and baby clothes, which were very long and tucked. Babies wore back flannels,[5] a long, sleeveless coat of warm cream flannel, with tapes attached at the back and tied in the front, and worn over the vest or chemise. The back flannels had pleats at the back and featherstitching in white silk. In winter we girls had red flannel petticoats.

There were no woollies, just worsted and woollen materials, out of which we had jackets and dresses, all handed down and made to fit.

In the evenings after the household chores were done we had to sew or crochet or make rugs. For rug making woollen scraps were cut up into strips by the younger ones and then with a hook the others pulled the strips through hessian and knotted them. Sometimes we used washed potato sacks opened out.

Mother taught us to make patchwork quilts and cushion covers from the smaller pieces of material from the rag bag and to embroider them along the joins with featherstitching.

We liked working together, as we would all sing and recite. Mother was a great singer and knew many old ballads and songs as well as hymns and psalms, and she would recite long poems, including Browning's The Pied Piper, Cowper's John Gilpin and

---

[5] Even I had one in 1910. - BM.

some of Eliza Cook's poems. We learnt these by heart, as well as Scriptures.

We would recite and sing all we learnt at school. My sister Nellie was shy and would not tell us what she had learnt, but would go and sit in the corner and recite under her breath.

We managed to hear her one day, when she thought no one was listening, and she was saying: "There was a cooked man, and he went a cooked mile, and found a cooked sixpence on a cooked stile. He bought a cooked cat, which caught a cooked mouse, and they all lived together in a little cooked house." "No," Mother said, "it's crooked." But she would stick to her own version.

Mother had a black flounced dress she wore in the winter. She liked lace collars in her later years and wore a cameo brooch. She could make lace and had several lace collars. In the summer she wore pink or lilac prints, which were afterwards cut down for us to wear. On weekdays she wore a paisley shawl, and a straw bonnet with a posy of flowers. In the winter she wore a black velvet cloak trimmed with bugles (long black beads) and a bonnet with berries.

Father wore either a moleskin or velvet waistcoat, and had a watch which sometimes had to be pawned. Mother hated such a thing and it was only done in dire circumstances, for instance when there was a doctor's bill to pay.

My maternal grandmother Sylvia had been one of Queen Victoria's needlewomen and did exquisite work, some of which Mother kept until her death. I remember a beautiful brown silk bodice, all hand made and embroidered with fleur de lis, and another in pink and green with forgetmenots and tiny rosebuds tied with bows of ribbon.

20. LOST IN THE FOG

One night it was very foggy, and the other children were all in bed. I stayed up to keep Mother company, and we were making a rag rug. I was cutting pieces.

But she got so worried about Father not being home, she sent me to bed and took the small tin lantern containing a candle for going outdoors, and went to look for him.

She lost her bearings and someone saw the light and shouted to her she had left the road and was in the field. They waited till she got on the road again and told her to go home. They were in a trap. She came back and soon Father came too.

It was good that the men saw her little light moving about and called to her or she might have fallen into the pond.

There were not many street lamps. We used to watch the old lamplighter come along and put up his lighter (a long taper fixed in a metal tube) to light the lamps and they were not very high.

Then some days he would come round with a little light ladder he used to carry, and his leather and cloth, and put the ladder on the cross bar of the lamp, and get up and clean the glass.

21. LAVENDER FROM MITCHAM

At Mitcham not very far away there were lavender fields and peppermint was grown. An old woman used to come round selling lavender. She wore a pair of men's boots, a black skirt green with age, a faded red blouse and a large black poke bonnet. Over her arm she had a large basket and she used to call: "Buy my sweet scented lavender! Sixteen good branches a penny."

In the autumn the same woman would come round, wearing a scarlet shawl, crying her peppermint cordial: "Have a little drop to keep your inside hot." If Mother could manage it she had a bottle to give us for various pains, or colds.

Then there was the fly paper man, who wore an old top hat with a sticky fly paper round it and a lot of flies. He used to call out: "Catch 'em all alive, nasty tormenting flies."

Sometimes a man came round with a barrow with a lot of what we called windmills, they were firewood sticks with thin cross pieces fixed with a pin and four little folded squares of coloured glossy paper, which whirled round in the wind. He did not sell them but exchanged them for clean jam jars.

In the winter a muffin man used to come round and ring a bell and call out: "Muffins for tea. Who'll have lovely hot muffins for tea?" He carried them in a basket on his head covered first with a white cloth, then a green baize one. He carried crumpets as well, which were cheaper.

In the summer a man and woman would come with a donkey cart selling shrimps, winkles, whelks and cockles. A penny bought half a pint of cockles or shrimps.

41

Every year a Frenchman came and sold onions, and in the summer Italians who sold ice cream and one had a barrel organ with a pathetic little monkey on top dressed in a red coat and blue trousers.

Once one of them came round with a dancing bear. We were rather nervous at first but the poor old bear danced round and round, the man sang some funny words (Italian). The bear looked cowed and hungry and his fur was moth eaten. The village children danced around it.

We used to watch from indoors, Mother would never let us play in the street.

Our postman used to come down the street with his sack on his back and would read the letters to those unable to do so themselves. In the summer we would hear him call out: "Mrs Harris, your son says on this postcard that he is coming to see you," or "Mrs Simpkins, your daughter had a baby girl on Wednesday." He would take our letters to the post. Postcards were cheap, and the postage stamp cost a half penny.

Alice aged 23

Ruth about 1913

43

22. YOU'LL BE LOCKED UP

We had to be very quiet. My father would be very stern and we knew we must not make any noise when he was home, though he never punished us, and my sister Ruth was the only one he smacked once because she sat by the cupboard door and he wanted to get something out and she would not get up, so he picked her up and smacked her.

She was rather spoilt because the babies that came after her died, and when my little brother was born she was very jealous for some time.

I remember before he was born one evening some children who were neighbours told us we could pick the white roses that hung over a fence. It was the garden of the cemetery manager and it backed on to the field.

We were delighted and picked some and took them indoors and put them in a jug of water as we thought Mother would like them. Then these children came to the door and called out: "You'll be locked up for stealing."

We were so frightened we put the jug of roses under the table and pulled down the blind, and got under the table ourselves, pulling the cloth down a bit to hide us. When Mother came home she wondered what was the matter. We told her we were so afraid a policeman would come and lock us all up before she came home.

Mother sent me to the manager's door with the roses and I was to say we were sorry and tell him how it had happened. He was so nice and kind, and told me never to pick any flowers unless the owner told me to, then he gave me a lovely bunch of sweet smelling white pinks.

23. KNEE SURGERY

After my little brother was born I used to nurse him and sing him to sleep, often carrying him up and down the room and I remember my father was annoyed when I sang the hymns I knew over and over again, as he liked to read his newspaper or book in the evening.

We only used oil lamps in those days and ours stood on the table and Father sat near the fire, and if I happened to get between him and the light he would say: "Sit down and be quiet." I would never let the baby cry and would nurse him for hours.

When Mother expected the next baby she had her bed brought downstairs. One evening she was sewing and I threaded some needles for her and put them on the table before I went on with mending the socks and stockings over a large wooden mushroom darner.

Presently Mother said one of the needles had dropped on the floor. I went down on my knees to look for it and felt a sharp prick. I said: "Oh dear it's gone into my knee."

I got up and there was only a red spot where it went in. Father put down his paper and looked and said: "Oh it's not in your knee." It had gone in between the bones in the kneecap and Mother thought she could get it out if she could get hold of the end, but it was no use and put me in more pain. In the end Father carried me up to bed and there I stayed till morning.

Then Mother got a strong neighbour to carry me to the doctor's, I was a thin child of 12. I was left at the doctor's and my legs up on two chairs, he probed and could feel the needle. He said: "You be good and when I've finished my visiting I will get it out." I was left alone in the strange room with its anatomical charts.

45

In the afternoon he gave me his handkerchief and told me to sniff well, and of course I lost consciousness, it was sprinkled with chloroform, and came round to find him putting a bandage on. In the dish there was the needle all except the eye, which was found on the carpet at home with the cotton threaded through it.

People often paid the doctor's bill at a few pennies a week, or gave him goods such as chickens and vegetables and even china ornaments and curios. One doctor managed to get quite a good collection of old china in this way.

After that there was the big flu epidemic and the Duke of Clarence died in January 1892, he was engaged to the Princess May as she was always called then. Afterwards she became engaged to the Duke of York, who became King George V and she was Queen Mary. I wrote in a little book a poem about it. Every verse ended: "So the Duke of York's to be married to the beautiful Princess May." Of course Queen Victoria was on the throne then.

So many people died in that epidemic. We had it mildly, and got over that, and then my little sister Grace Rebecca was born, she became my care and I always called her my baby. She even slept beside me. She was such a lovely little thing and I never wanted to leave her.

24. GHOSTS AT CHURCH SERVICE

I must put down our early experience of going to church. We had always gone to the mission hall, which was known locally by the text over it as God is Love, and some children living near us persuaded us to try the church, saying it was so much better.

So I and my sister Agnes went one Sunday morning. We went into the church and sat down together in a seat. Two ladies came in and looked surprised. They said: "You cannot sit here, children, this is our pew."

The same thing happened again but we got a seat at last, and sitting very quietly, presently we saw some white robed figures came in from the end of the church.

As the church was surrounded by the churchyard and we had never seen men robed like that, both thought they had risen from the graves. We clung to one another in silence and were relieved when we saw them turn and sit in their seats in the choir. We thought it so strange and as we had never seen surplices concluded they came in their nightshirts.

We saw the other children after and told them we did not like it. They said: "Oh you should come to Sunday school this afternoon and then you would go into church with all the children." So in the afternoon we went, but that seemed worse to me.

We were put into a class and the teacher said: "What is your name?" I said: "Alice Mary." She said: "Who gave you that name?" I said: "My mother." She said: "You must say, 'my godfathers and godmothers in my baptism' [the Catechism response]."

"No,"I said "that's not true, because my mother told me she gave me my name." When I went home I said, "I don't want to go to that church and Sunday school." I did not like it as they wanted me to tell untruths.

Our own Sunday school was much farther to go, but I loved that Sunday school. I expect Mother let us try the other because it was nearer.

My little prizes I received for learning the text and verse each week, I kept, except my New Testament which I gave to one of the girls at the fever hospital, as I wanted her to read it. This was when I was about 20. The Acts of the Apostles, illustrated, I gave my son and he passed it on to my grandson.

25. CHILDREN QUEUE FOR STALE BREAD

There were some little old fashioned courts, one called Angel Court, a square with houses round, and Browns Court, and Salvador. The shops were very old fashioned. Some of them you had to go down a step to enter and some up three steps.

At Tooting Broadway were several nice shops. At the corner of High Street and Defoe Road some German people named Jung kept a bakery. Every morning saw a queue of poor children outside waiting for stale bread and cakes. When we lived near the pond in the house where my brother was born Mother sent two of us to join the queue and we used to get up early. My father was at Margate and we had so little to live on. For 3d [3 pennies or just over 1p] we got a pillow case full of stale bread and buns.

Sometimes if Mother could spare a penny we asked for a pennyworth of cake crumbs, and got a good measure of pieces of cake and pastries and broken biscuits. Oh they were a treat!

The baker's wife was very generous and when we thanked her she would just nod her head and say: "Tis nutting." She had a round face, and she wore a dark dress and a large white apron with a bib.

A butcher's shop was near by, with sides of meat hanging up and a marble slab as well as the wooden chopping blocks, and lots of sawdust on the floor.

One day Mother sent me to this butcher to buy a piece of belly pork. I was too shy to go in and ask for it, as I thought it was rude to say 'belly', so I loitered about outside.

Along came my sister Ruth and said she did not mind asking for it. She bounced into the shop and said: "She wants a piece of pork with buttons on," which made the butcher laugh and embarrassed me still more. After that we called it Ruth's 'button shop'.

At the corn chandler's shop we used to get bran and middlings for the fowls. It was always a dusty place as the goods were kept in sacks and open bins and weighed out into open scales with big metal scoops.

The chemist had an old dark shop with three enormous glass bottles in the window filled with coloured liquids which glowed like jewels. One was red, one blue and one green. He rolled his own pills. We used to go there for a pennyworth of gripe water for the babies.

Inside were advertisements for patent medicines, many of which offered to get rid of unwanted fat. One showed a very stout lady struggling to get into her carriage and being pushed up from behind by a little groom, who appeared to be perspiring with the effort.

Directly you went into the haberdasher and draper's a bell tinkled and the floor walker cried out to the assistants: "Miss Smith, or Miss Brown, forward please," and they had to hurry out to serve us. We did not buy much but everything was priced to end in farthings, eleven pennies three farthings etc.

When we asked Mother why this was, she said it made the goods seem cheaper than if the price was rounded up to the nearest shilling. The assistant would always ask: "Will you take the farthing [in change] or a packet of pins?" We generally had to ask for the farthing.

Many hats on display had extraordinary trimmings, bird's wings, flower gardens, quills from porcupines, lace, velvet, tulle and ribbons. They were in various types of straw and Mother could tell which was which, as the village women at her home had sat in their doorways making straw plait to be taken to Luton, centre of the straw hat trade.

Near our house was a corner grocery shop. The owners were named Catt, and had been childless for years when they suddenly produced a son. They were delighted and without forethought they named him Thomas. The poor child suffered for it when he went to school.

Aggie when she was with the Shirley Schools, 1900's

26. CHRISTMAS

Christmas was a time of happiness and excitement. We could not afford a tree but Mother got a big branch of fir for a penny. She put it in a barrel of earth and we hung on it coloured paper rosettes we made from wrappings saved up during the year, and stars and moons cut from tin foil. We also hung up a few striped candy walking sticks which Mother bought.

We each made little presents for all the family. There were needle cases and pin cushions made from scraps of silk and velvet which had come in the rag bag. For Father there would be a pair of slippers worked in Berlin wool, for Mother a bag for her sewing. For Bertie we painted and dressed wooden clothes pegs to look like soldiers.

In our stocking toes there were always a few nuts saved from Uncle Jim's visit, and an orange. One Christmas I received a paintbox and thus began a lifelong pleasure.

We went to the paper mill to get coloured offcuts which we made into paper chains with paste made of flour and hot water. We searched the hedges for a bit of holly and sometimes were lucky enough to find a piece of mistletoe which had been dropped by the Gypsies, who brought their lace and wares around just before Christmas as people were in a more liberal frame of mind then.

The grocer displayed windows full of dried fruit and candied peel in large heaps. I never could understand why the currants were labelled 'Fine bold currants' as they were so small I wondered what made them bold. Great japanned tins of tea read Finest Indian, or Ceylon, or China, as the case might be.

There were jars of preserved ginger in beautiful blue and white Chinese ware, and boxes of preserved fruit from abroad, open to show the luscious pears, plums and apricots in their glazed coverings. Inside there were casks of syrup and black treacle. We used to buy two pennyworth, to go with our suet puddings and to put in a fruit cake if Mother could manage to make one.

The poulterer and butcher hung his wares up outside, festooned with coloured paper and each bird decorated with a rosette.

We used to go to a Christmas service early, then help Mother cook the dinner. She generally got a nice piece of beef by queueing up till just before the butcher's shop shut, when he would sell meat cheaply as there was not enough space to keep it in his ice store before the days of freezers. We always had to get our meat late on Saturdays when the richer people had taken the best cuts, and there were usually free bones to be had for soup.

As we had our own vegetables we could have a nice dinner with a plum pudding, not a rich one, to follow. After dinner we washed up and read or admired our presents and played guessing games with Mother. Then she would sing old ballads to us. We liked them to be doleful and one sad temperance song by Henry Clay Work never failed to move us. One verse went:

Father, dear father, come home with me now!
The clock in the steeple strikes one;
You promis'd, dear father, that you would come home,
As soon as your day's work was done;
Our fire has gone out - our house is all dark -
And mother's been watching since tea,
With poor brother Benny so sick in her arms,
And no one to help her but me.
Come home, come home, come home,
Please, father, dear father, come home.

The wretched man was out drinking all night and the baby died. We did not question why the child called him dear father.

Father liked to hear us sing when he was not reading. Sometimes he would go for a walk in the evening, just before we all turned in.

Pat with his first wife, Hannah, son David and daughter Norah, 1890's

27. EASTER EGGS

At Easter time the churches and chapels were all decorated with spring flowers, and the boys and girls used to walk in twos with posies of violets, primroses and wallflowers, an Easter parade. Sometimes their flowers were taken up to the front inside the parish church and put down near the altar.

We used to go and look for cowslips, if Easter was late, and forgetmenots and kingcups. People began to wear lighter clothes, and buy new hats and bonnets or refurbish old ones.

At home we used to take it in turns having the top off Father's boiled egg, when one day my sister Ruth asked why we could not have a whole egg apiece. Mother said that when eggs were 24 a shilling [5p] we should.

This time came one Easter and Mother bought the eggs, then showed us how to cut out our initials in paper and bind them to the eggs with onion skins, and boil them hard. When cold we peeled off the skins and there were our own initials, standing out, and the eggs had gone a lovely dark brown. For herself Mother had done tiny fern leaves and for Father a small ivy leaf. We were enchanted with the result and did not want to eat them.

Hot cross buns were two a penny but Mother would get brewer's balm (yeast) and bake her own. These we had hot for breakfast and again for tea on Good Friday. Generally our breakfast was bread and beef dripping, or toast. Occasionally we had porridge or stir about, which was made of flour and skim milk. Tea being a more expensive item we had the weak kind known as cambric.

May Day was a great occasion. At school the children were taught how to dance round the maypole, and a large pole was erected on the green and to the top were fastened coloured ribbons. The children stood in a circle and each was given an end to hold, then as they danced they interwove the ribbons. It was a very pretty sight.

Next came the crowning of the May Queen. A young girl dressed in white with her long hair loose was crowned with a beautiful wreath of flowers in which was entwined hawthorn blossom. We loved to recite Tennyson's poem The May Queen about the girl who was to be Queen o' the May and who told her mother to wake and call her early.

The children had a day's holiday from school, and the men were given flowers to wear in their buttonholes, the women had bunches of flowers and the little girls had flowers tucked behind their ears. Sometimes there was tea on the green and the children all brought their own mugs, and were given buns and flat spicy May cakes.

28. HOUSEHOLD CHORES

Household chores were sheer hard work. In some of the houses we lived in we had cold water laid on, either to the scullery or to a tap outside. In others we had to use a well or spring which was shared with neighbours. Every house had a copper in the washhouse or scullery, many had a low brown stone sink, and there was either a small fireplace or an iron range to be blackleaded every day.

Liquid blacking was brushed on the ironwork and then polished with a polishing brush. The hearthstone had to be whitened and also the front step with a lump of chalky whitening. The stone was washed, whitening spread on it and evenly washed and left to dry. In those houses which had cellars there was also a coal chute with an iron coal hole cover which needed blackleading. Coal was necessary for both warmth and cooking.

The copper was about 3-4 ft high and 3-4 ft wide. It had an iron pan, with a tap and a heavy wooden lid, and was built around with bricks and cemented into a wall, generally an outside wall, with a space underneath where the fire was lit, and a chimney. The lid had to be scrubbed after the wash.

Not only was washing boiled in the copper but also hot water for baths, which were taken in galvanised baths big enough to sit in with your knees drawn up, usually a Saturday night ritual.

Christmas puddings were boiled in the copper and anyone fortunate enough to have a piece of bacon or ham too big for a saucepan popped that in, though not at the same time! Scullery floors were tiled or made of stone flags, though some were boarded, and all had to be scrubbed with the soapy water when the laundry was done, just as Mother did on her wedding day after her landlady's baby was born.

57

The floors and stairs were kept scrubbed and a scrubbing brush was an important feature in our household. We had several. One was for hands and knees, which we should now call a nail brush. One was for scrubbing clothes and a much larger one was for floors. When we were little we often wished this was smaller, for us to grasp properly.

Clothes were washed by hand with hard soap, often home made from rendered fat and wood ashes, plus a touch of blue,[6] boiled and allowed to harden before being cut up and stored. We had a scrubbing board as well as the scrubbing brush for the dirtier clothes. Certain clothes could be boiled after scrubbing, nothing that would shrink.

Household linen, all white things, was boiled in the copper. More delicate things were never scrubbed or boiled. They were washed with flaked soap, made by grating the bar of soap into warm water using a suet grater.

Tea was used to rinse ecru lace collars and curtains, and tea leaves were scattered in moist heaps on the pieces of carpet, then swept up with a dustpan and a hard brush. They made the colours bright, as dust and fluff clung to them, and quite often were used on Turkey carpets.

The kitchen was the warmest room for there was a good fire in the range for cooking and generally a big fireguard, which we often used during Saturday bath nights to air the clean clothes that we wore on Sundays. The ironing was done there and we had a goose-necked iron, some sad (flat) irons and a goffering iron which were kept hot on top of the stove and tested by holding up near the cheek. Woe betide us if we scorched anything.

---

[6] Blue in a bag, still available in old ironmongers' and a modern version in some shops. It was used for getting clothes white and put into the rinsing water. - BM.

58

Our pride was a large mangle which Mother acquired second hand. It stood on a red and green base and had a large wheel at the right hand side with a handle to turn the rollers. There was a large screw on top to tighten the rollers. When we bought it Mother said: "Now we're on the pig's back."

We could put wet things through to save wringing by hand, and dry sheets and towels would be pressed quite smoothly if they had been evenly folded first.

We had heavy iron saucepans for cooking and, except for a tin one once, an iron kettle as it had to sit over the fire for a quick boil. Toast was made in front of the fire on a three pronged toasting fork with a long handle.

There were two old Windsor armchairs, one for each parent. We children sat on a bench or on stools. Father made these and it was lovely to sit on them and look for faces and castles in the fire.

Sheets were darned and patched, and turned sides to middle as I have explained. Bleached cotton or twill was more expensive than the unbleached kind, so we generally had unbleached twill, which washed white after frequent laundering. Candles were our only light upstairs. Some people fortunate enough to have moulds made their own. The poorest floated a wick in some oil and made a tiny lamp in a small vessel with a spout.

Sweeping was done with a hard broom, a soft hair broom, and hard and soft hand brushes. Furniture was polished with beeswax. We used a lump of soda for washing greasy dishes, knife powder for cleaning knives and whitening for polishing silver. Saucepans were scoured with sand. Steel fire irons and fenders were rubbed with emery paper. Mother had a Greek key pattern steel fender and fire irons which had to be kept shining.

There was a great deal of mending. Socks and stockings were knitted and the socks had to be refooted if they were past darning but the legs still good. It seemed as if we were always mending and making do. Coats had to be unpicked and turned, dresses let out or taken up and the hems faced, all by hand.

Mother told us it was no disgrace to be poor but it was to be dirty or ragged. A lady could appear with a patch or a darn but a hole or unmended tear betokened poor housekeeping and low standards. We went out in gloves with the fingers darned and, as we later discovered, many of the richer people thought no shame of doing likewise as long as they were neat.

Hair had to be brushed and braided. Mother abhorred slovenliness and kept herself very neat and tidy. Every child had a handkerchief and was made to use it. She could not abide sniffing.

When there was a death in the family everyone wore something black, even if it was only an armband or a diamond sewn on to the left sleeve. Full mourning for a very near relative was observed for six months and half mourning, greys and lavender shades, for the next six. Widows wore veils known as weeds. I remember how long some of them were.

Mother said it was false modesty for people to wear such elaborate shows of mourning except for royalty, whose tearful faces needed protection from the gaze of the public. She was very cross when my sister Ruth wore long weeds after the death of her first husband.

If we had one the parlour, or sitting room as we called it, was used for entertaining. Some of the friends Mother had before she married would visit and take a cup of tea. Mother loved nice china and would buy oddments cheaply, if sets were broken in the shops, and keep these for company.

We were taught to say what were known as party pieces, poems learnt and recited to visitors, but we could never go into the parlour unless sent for and we had to curtsy, answer politely any questions and leave again at a nod from Mother. We were not supposed to be in the room when there was adult conversation.

At meals there was always a clean tablecloth and places had to be set properly. We had to speak when we were spoken to. Mother kept a stick on the table to correct us and we could not ask for food, but had to wait till it was given to us and there was never a time when we were allowed to take food in our hands and go off to eat it.

When all were served we said grace. When we had finished we had to say another grace and then ask: "Please, Mother, may I get down?"

One visitor we loved was cousin Victoria, Father's brother Benjamin's daughter. She was a companion and had a quaint elegance. Her visits were always unexpected and she never went without leaving a surprise, like a fairy godmother. Bonbons from Fortnum and Mason's in Piccadilly, London, Christmas crackers, fancy biscuits, and once glace fruits in a large wooden box.

In the parlour many people had festoons over everything, and there were sashes to tie back the curtains, and antimacassars on the armchairs to prevent the men soiling them with their greasy hair. Knick knacks abounded, many displayed on shelved stands known as whatnots. People brought back crested china trinkets from places they visited. Walls were covered in portraits and pictures.

The walls had dark wallpaper as a rule, many in dark red, brown or green, with formal (non floral) patterns, and paintwork was dark too, graining and varnishing considered stylish.

Our parlour was less fussy. Mother made up permanganate of potash solution and stained the boards round the square of Brussels carpet someone had given us, and there were rugs and dyed serge curtains.

There was a high mantelshelf, with a scalloped tapestry pelmet, and on this was my father's clock and two green glass ornaments with glass prisms dangling and reflecting the light. There were some nice vases and pictures, and embroidered cloths.

Our bedrooms were papered in lighter wallpaper, generally with a floral design. I remember one of cabbage roses. The papering was done by my parents, with flour and water paste. We children had to cut the edges off the rolls of paper, ready for them to paste on the kitchen table.

Up in the bedrooms there was the marble topped washstand. Ours were bought second hand for a shilling or two. On the marble slab were a jug and basin. We had to wash in our bedrooms in cold water, even in the winter, often having first to break the ice on top. Then the dirty water would be poured into a slop pail and carried downstairs to be emptied.

The bedroom floors were of scrubbed boards save for, usually, a home made rag rug at the side of the bed. It was thought to be a great thing to have linoleum or a piece of carpet.

Most poor people had palliasses to lie on or mattresses of flock. This was woollen waste. The mattresses were sometimes made at home but generally bought. Flock was always getting lumpy and once a week it had to be smoothed out with the fingers, a very tedious job. As soon as Mother had enough breast feathers from her chickens she made a feather bed for herself and Father.

She had feather pillows at the time of her marriage but as the family increased the children had to make do with flock pillows.

Alice (far left) at the infirmary at the Shirley Schools, 1900's

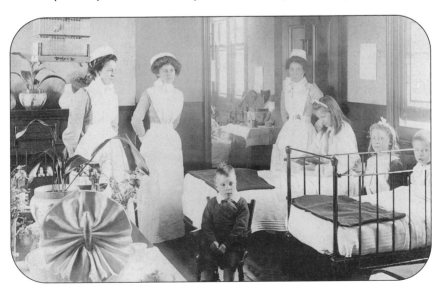

30. BABY GRACE DIES

When dear little baby Grace was eight months old Mother was taken ill and I tried to carry on. I remember doing some of the washing and I had the care of the others and the baby night and day.

Then one morning I went to the butcher's to get some shin of beef to make beef tea, which we did by simmering the beef in seasoned water in a galleypot (a handleless pot) on the hob for several hours.

Coming back I could not walk straight. I tried to keep near a very high wall, but found myself stumbling about in the middle of the road. I managed to get home and get upstairs.

I stood by Mother's bed shaking and feeling so strange. I can remember during the previous night thinking someone was taking the baby and I was continually having to hold her. No doubt I was ill then.

My sister Aggie put some bedclothes on the small chairbed in Mother's room and I lay down. When the doctor came to see Mother he said I was ill with a severe bout of influenza and must be kept in bed.

Mother had the baby in with her, but Aggie had to do the things I usually did. But the baby's bottle was not washed properly and Mother ill, she gave her the bottle and when she took the stopper out she knew the milk had turned sour.

Poor baby! she was teething and was ill with diarrhoea and sickness about 10 days, and then died. Oh how I missed her, she was always my baby, and I had carried her everywhere, my arms felt empty.

One day after I was better the School Board summoned one or other of my parents to appear and explain why my sister Nellie had been absent. Nellie had a weak heart and every year she suffered with chilblains.

Both Mother and Father were at work and Mother decided I would have to go. She tied up the waist of one of her long dresses, put her shawl round my shoulders, a big straw bonnet tied under my chin and a pair of black cotton gloves on my hands.

In the Board room an old gentleman with whiskers said: "Are you this child's mother?" I hung my head, so no doubt he took it for consent, berated me and dismissed me. I was so afraid they would find out that I too had not been to school when I should have been.

Nellie, aged 28

31. IN SERVICE

Soon after this Mother took me to Defoe Road to live with an elderly lady, named Mrs Meeking. She had long greyish curls dangling each side of her face and her head was constantly shaking. She had a high pitched voice and would dart out little moral remarks but was very parsimonious. She wore a brown pleated dress and black apron, and elastic sided boots.

Her husband was a quiet dark haired man who preached at some services but was mostly at home, reading and writing in his study. He rarely addressed me.

It was very strange to me. They used the dining room in front of the house, the drawing room was unused but kept dusted and then locked up. There was a big rather empty kitchen with a big black grate, never used, no matter how cold it might be, a big dresser along one side and on the top shelf were basins in which Mrs Meeking put the cream off the milk each day.

The old scullery next to the kitchen had a little fire. In the corner was a copper and a tap over, which was tied up with rags so that it should not be used. Mrs Meeking thought it might leak and waste water.

I did the sweeping and dusting and washing up, laid the table and helped make the beds. Upstairs there was a small room, in which there was an oil stove with an oven. We had to make Allinson's wholemeal bread and bake it up there once a week.

They did not believe in meat and used to eat a lot of fruit and nuts and I had to go shopping with her and carry the things. I was given brown bread and apples for breakfast, and told brown bread and apples were the best things to put in the stomach.

When there was enough cream I had to put it in a wide mouthed bottle and cork it and then by a constant shaking make it into butter.

One day we had been out shopping and it was very cold. She told me to come into the dining room where there was a little fire and shake the bottle. She was counting up what she had spent. She kept asking me: "Was that fippence or fippence farthing?" She could not pronounce her Rs.

I was getting tired of shaking the bottle and my hands were cold and stiff. Suddenly the bottle flew out of my hands and a stream of buttermilk and curds in its wake. She screamed: "Weuben, Weuben! Come and see what this dweadful[7] girl has done."

I truly felt dreadful, and was scolded so that I cried. Then after clearing it up she said she would take me home to Mother, but as my eyes were red she tied a veil over my face, as she said people might think she had been beating me. It seemed though she wanted me to stay until she got an older girl.

She engaged my mother to come and do the washing once and there was four months' laundry to be done. Mrs Meeking had sheets, blankets and towels done only three times a year. A woman came once a month to do the smalls.

It was winter and I was called very early and told I was to go out to the coachhouse at the back of the house and climb on a stool to dip up buckets of rain water from the large butt outside it and fill the copper. I was very nervous of that coachhouse, as it was still dark and I thought I heard rats. I remember the moon and the stars and how deep the sky looked, I had never been out alone in the dark or so early.

---

[7] The notebook has 'awful' but Alice said Mrs Meeking said 'dweadful'. - BM.

I was afraid of the dark, but I looked up at the sky and suddenly I thought that God was up there and He was looking down kindly on me.

I had to have the water boiling for the wash. Sometimes I had to break the ice and the buckets were too heavy for me so I spilt some and splashed myself with the icy water.

Some days Mrs Meeking gave me a leather and dusters and I had to clean the windows of the drawing room on the first floor. She tied a rope round my waist and the other end to her left wrist. While I sat out on the sill she walked round the room dusting her ornaments with her right hand. I think if I had fallen she would have followed, she was very slim and shaky.

My bedroom was next to hers on the top floor, and when I went to bed she said I must take everything off and shake it out on the landing. In the morning I had to take everything off my bed and shake it out on the landing, and do the same with hers. She had some strange fancies. Her husband slept in a room below.

One day while I was helping her make her husband's bed, she looked at me and said, quoting from one of her husband's sermons: "The Lord will not return until the Jews are back in their own land." I was so surprised. I had never heard anything like this and could not understand what it meant, Jerusalem seemed far away and I knew the Jews were scattered in other lands, and I had never heard about the Lord returning.

One afternoon my sisters came to the house and called to me through the letter box that Mother had made a bread pudding for tea. Mrs Meeking was having a nap up in the drawing room, so I scribbled a note and went off with the girls to have tea at home. Mother scolded me and told me not to do it again, but gave me some pudding.

69

After a while Mrs Meeking said I was too thin to do all she wanted. As she only paid me 2 shillings a week I hardly think she could have got more for her money, but I was given my wages and sent home to Mother.

The next day I was allowed to go to Jung's the baker's with a pillow case and get 3d worth of stale bread and cake. It was full and we called it my homecoming feast.

Alice and Pat's son, Len, at nine months

I was home again for a little while, and then my Sunday school teacher heard of an opening. It was for a nurse girl. Mother took me one evening to Balham, to a big old house in Fontenoy Road to see the lady. She thought me very young but Mother told her I was quite used to the care of babies and I was engaged. It was all very strange to me.

I went in the evening and did not see the baby who was nine months old. Our darling Grace was about the same age when she died and was such a wonderful baby, bright and knowing. I looked forward to caring for this one. I was sent to sleep in the schoolroom on a camp bed the first night, and told the lady help would call me in the morning and I was to go down to the nursery and stay with the baby until her mother came to tell me about her bath.

I went down to find a very stolid baby who just stared, and although I tried to get her to smile or be interested she remained dumb to all my advances. I was told to get the bath and towels etc, her mother bathed her and I was told to go up and help the two little boys to dress.

There were two girls, they were the eldest, one my age and one older, then a boy at boarding school and the two little boys Peter and Claude. They had a morning governess and then I had to take them out.

But to begin that morning I carried the baby down to the dining room, the breakfast was laid and all the family assembled, so I was told to go down to the kitchen and have mine. The lady help had hers with the family. She was a poor relation who acted as a sort of companion and did the cooking, though she was a poor cook. I went down the bare stairs.

Oh what a dismal place. There was a big kitchen but hardly anything in it. I had to look round for something to eat and found part of a loaf and some butter, no cup and saucer, only a big mug,[8] and on the stove part of an old coffee pot with some tea in it. It was lonely and miserable. I managed to cut some bread and butter, but the place smelt of mice, and musty. I did not know then that there were big rat holes in the skirting boards.

The lady help was very strange. She did not speak to me unless obliged, and did not answer when I spoke to her. She relayed messages from the mistress. After breakfast I had to take the baby out in her pram on the common and was told to come back at eleven for her to have a bottle, and then I would have to take the little boys as well because they would have finished their lessons.

It seemed a long morning as the baby remained so stolid and I thought it must be time so I returned too early. I had no means of knowing the time.

But although the boys were rather tiresome and naughty, they were lively and interesting to talk to and became very fond of me. They would call me Pit-a-Pat, and on Sunday when I put on my best frock to go home they would shout out: "Pit-a-Pat in full trim."

The baby soon brightened up. I used to sing nursery rhymes to her when I put her to sleep and when I was out Sunday afternoon and evening her elder sisters used to do this, but they could not get her to sleep.

---

[8] A jam jar. - BM.

One Sunday evening I was in and the lady help out and I was told to lay the table for supper. I went down the stairs but when I got into the kitchen I heard such strange rustlings and squeakings, I was frightened and ran back. The little boys said: "Oh it's only the rats," and they stamped on the stairs while I got the supper things on a tray and took it up to the dining room.

Mr Bowen was a doctor, but not of medicine, he was engaged in study. He used to go out each morning, but was home most of the time. He was a strange man, and when my month's money was due, it was 10 shillings as I earned 2/6 [2 shillings 6 pennies] a week, I had to ask him for it. He would give me the half sovereign and my sisters who had called for it would take it home to Mother.

After the first night, I slept in an attic room in an old double bed and one night it rained and came through on the bed, so I kept to the side where it was dry. When I had been there a month and had no change of sheet or pillow case, I told Mother and she said: "You must ask for a clean sheet."

Everything was the same. The mistress used to sit reading novels all day, matters were left to the lady help and things were terribly neglected.

They were looking for another house and decided on one being built. We moved into it before it was quite finished, and I remember how much I did or overdid. There was a great deal of clearing up to be done, but no one seemed to take charge. Mother was engaged to help and sweep up the old house, I had a bad attack of biliary colic to end the day and had to go to bed.

I was with them about six months and might have been longer, but they had influenza and one very wet night I was sent to an out of the way place to get them some new laid eggs. It was dark and unmade roads and no lights. The rain poured down and the dogs barked and I was scared. I was wet through when I got back and my legs were muddy.

In a few days I felt so ill and could only sit about and mind the baby. They decided to send me home so when the laundry cart came, they asked the man to take me with him.

I sat up beside him in the open cart, and when we reached our house, he said: "Your young girl is ill." My father had to carry me upstairs as I could not walk. I had rheumatic fever.

When I got better I had to go to another place, and they gave me so little food, life was very hard, and then to another place as bad. I had dinner given me with big maggots in, crawling out of an old bacon[9] bone boiled with an onion and carrot to make stew. I ran away, calling through the letter box that I was off.

Mother told me that this was impolite and I should have spoken for my release to the lady, not been afraid to speak out. I told her the rest of the house was filthy except for the parlour. The woman was deaf and very short sighted. Perhaps she ate maggots and did not notice them. She did not seem to see the dirt everywhere.

---

[9] We should say ham bone. - BM.

33. BLESSED ASSURANCE 1895

One day when I was 15 I was on my knees cleaning the kitchen floor and thinking of the Lord and the man who came to the disciples with his son who was dumb and had terrible fits. They could not help so he asked Jesus. I could almost see the Lord and the poor man and hear the Lord say: "If thou canst believe, all things *are* possible to him that believeth," and hear the man cry "Lord, I believe; help Thou my unbelief" (Mark 9 v 23-24).

I said: "Oh that is it, there is some unbelief in my heart," so I too cried: "Lord, I believe; help thou my unbelief," and such a light shone into my soul, such an assurance, it has been mine for 62 years. Oh the wonder of it. I never remember the time when I did not desire to belong to the Lord, but did not understand.

I thought my sisters would be glad to know how wonderful it was, but no! My sister Ruth just said: "Oh you were born religious," so I found no understanding.

A few years after, I wrote many letters to my sister Nellie and prayed for her. When I took her to Gypsy Smith's mission she did stand up to the appeal, then she went away and she joined a chapel, and later got in touch with a church woman and was confirmed. I believe she had faith in the Lord, but would never talk about spiritual things.

She was a dear loving sister and died after an operation at 63. My other sisters seem hard and unrepentant. I still pray for them, they are both well over 70.

Now I must go on from my blessed experience. I went to the little chapel, it was Wesleyan and I joined the Bible class. How I did enjoy that class, and when the Sunday school superintendent and his wife were leaving Tooting for Bromley, Kent, my sister Nellie was in service with them. But Mother thought she was too young to go so far from home, so I had to go and see Mrs Newman and tell her.

I wished I could go instead. Then there seemed to be so many obstacles in the way, but I prayed about it and the Lord opened up the way, and Mrs Newman asked me to go in Nellie's place.

Oh I was happy to be with Christian people. They were such a lovely family, polite and affectionate, and the home was well run. There were eight children, I loved them all and two of the little girls especially. We had happy times. We used to share the chores, for all the children helped. If we finished early I used to read to them and talk about the Lord.

We went for walks and played dressing up games. For years I had a photo of them pretending to be a wedding group, with the bride veiled in one of the lace curtains from the dining room.

Oh the joy when Olive told me she had given her heart to the Lord and then Hilda the next day. We used to sing and say our prayers together at night.

Before that I had the wonderful joy and experience of leading another girl to the Lord. Mrs Newman expected her sister and husband and their little daughter and maid to stay a few days, on their way to a new home at Sidcup. Knowing the little maid would sleep in my room I began to pray for her, and the first night when we went to bed we had not had any conversation on spiritual things.

I could not get to sleep as I felt I ought to have spoken to her, so I got out of bed to pray. Presently she woke and asked what I was doing. She said: "You said your prayers before you got into bed." "Yes," I said, "but I'm praying for you, that you may know the Lord and give your heart to Him." She said: "Oh that is what I want," and got out of bed to kneel beside me, she was longing to know the way.

We were so happy and had so much to talk about, that we did not think of the time and soon heard a knocking on the ceiling in the room below from my mistress.

I was very young and now I think how she would have rejoiced if I had told her what had happened in her house that night. There was joy in heaven over a soul born again. Dear Amy I kept in touch with her for years, some glad day we shall meet again. 'What a gathering of the ransomed that will be.'

The next year another baby was born, and the woman who came as nurse upset us. She was very deceitful. I did not know but she was saying untrue things about me to upset the mistress, that I was not doing all I could, and saying to me I ought to have a better place, as it seemed she wanted the post for one of her relatives.

So by the time she left we were not very happy but I got over this and poor Mrs Newman had a relapse and I took over washing and dressing the dear baby. They named her Margery Alice, the second name for me. I did all the washing, cooking and cleaning I could till Mrs Newman recovered. My time with her was the happiest I had known.

When I was 19 I went to a fever hospital in Tooting and soon after my sister Agnes came. While I was there a tent mission started, and I got some of the staff to go. I believe some were really converted and I was in touch with some for a few years.

After a time at the fever hospital which I had to leave because of my varicose veins, I was recommended by the doctor to go to St Thomas's, London, for an operation, and after going up and down and waiting for a bed, I had to give up and start work as I could not go on without any money.

Mrs Hampton. The picture was sent to Alice's Mother by Mrs Hampton's daughter Gwen when Mrs Hampton died in June 1925

34. NURSE AT CLAPHAM VICAR'S

I went as nurse to a first baby at Clapham Common, the father was the vicar at St Barnabas'. He was so pleased with the child he had the doctor circumcise and vaccinate him too soon.

The poor mite was allergic to something and presently he was covered with a rash which turned to eczema. He had to be carried round on a pillow and I got no rest day or night as he wailed continually.

Then the cook had flu and the housemaid left. I had to do such a lot for a few days and I found the cook had been throwing good food away and lots of things were amiss, but she came from the mistress's Hampshire home, and she thought her a wonderful maid.

After she was able to work again I was feeling ill but tried to carry on with the housework and the baby till one morning I was so feverish and in such pain I could not stand. It was Sunday and the mistress sent for the doctor.

He said it looked like rheumatic fever, so he tried to get me into hospital, but they had no bed, so the vicar ordered a cab and carried me downstairs and put me in and sent me home. This was Sunday evening.

My sister Ruth came to the door, and exclaimed: "Mother it's Alice." The cab man carried me into the front room, and Mother made up a little bed for me. Next day our doctor came, and it was not rheumatic fever, but very bad influenza and I was very run down.

35. WHAT A TRIAL THESE WOMEN ARE

When I got better the doctor said I ought not to have heavy work but something light and asked if I would like to go to his house, the Waterfall. There was only the doctor as he was a bachelor, the housekeeper was an elderly woman and he needed someone younger to help with answering the door, and looking after the surgery and the patients.

We each had a bedroom at the top of the house. There was only the one bedroom occupied on the floor below and that was the doctor's, then there was a stairway from the end of the back hall which led to the flat used by the coachman.

When the other doctor lived there his coachman was a married man with children but after he went to Balham his partner Dr Shaw was left at the Waterfall. Dr Shaw had a young man named John as coachman and he had one room in the flat for a bedroom. There was a dispenser who came daily.

It was a lovely old house and garden, and the hall especially with a big fireplace and two big figures of armour each side of it in which it would have been easy for anyone to hide. Water splashed down over some rocks in the garden, giving the house its name. I could have been quite happy and comfortable there, but again I soon saw things were wrong.

Doctor used to give me money to pay bills and I wondered at the amount, as I knew we did not consume so much butter etc. There were big cellars and larders etc and one day I had to go into the one the butter was kept in and saw quite a lot.

After the housekeeper went out I went in again and the butter had gone, other things too. I let her know I noticed things and she was very nasty and made everything uncomfortable for me. I was

80

wondering what to do, when the lady housekeeper at Balham at Dr Taylor's rang and asked me to come up. I told her about things and she said quite apart from that Mrs Wareham had spread false things about and the servants and others had heard, and she asked me if I had been told anything so I said: "Yes." She said: "You are young and this is nothing to do with you, but Mrs Wareham will be leaving."

The next morning Dr Taylor's carriage drove in and the coachman and the doctor came in. Both doctors and the two coachmen were in the dining room and Mrs Wareham was sent for, and when she came out she went up and packed her things and went.

Dr Shaw asked me if I could get a woman to do the cleaning and someone to come and sleep with me until he could get another housekeeper. I did and managed until the new housekeeper came.

She had been engaged by the lady housekeeper at Balham, Dr Taylor's housekeeper. His wife died at the Waterfall, leaving him with some little girls. The maids and their coachman had been with them for years and Mrs Blair, the housekeeper, was a widow and looked after everything.

Well this new one for Dr Shaw's soon proved a failure. She used to hurry down in the morning and go into doctor's breakfast room and open the shutters. This was nothing to do with her, and then I noticed the smell of spirits and soon noticed the whiskey was going fast, so I told the doctor.

He said: "Oh dear, what a trial these women are, and we have to have one, as I'm young, and you are young, and John is young, and so we must have someone who is older to live in the house."

Another thing soon happened. The housekeeper's niece came early one morning before we were up. I went down and let her in

81

and she went up to her aunt's bedroom. Soon the house rang with hysterical screaming. I did not go up and hoped the doctor would not be upset. After a time they both came down dressed to go out and the niece just said her mother has died.

I got on with things and when the doctor came down he said: "What's all the screaming about?" so I told him. I did not know when to expect her back and had no word from her, but on the Saturday evening back she came and a load of furniture. She had not asked the doctor for permission, and had it put up in the empty rooms upstairs, as the drawing room and nursery were unfurnished.

She soon was drinking heavily and the doctor said: "This won't do," so she was given notice, and then the next one came. She was a martinet and she evidently meant to get *her* niece there. I knew the doctor and his ways and did all his rooms and took the phone messages, but she interfered and upset everything, so I had to tell doctor I could not stay with her.

It was as I thought. She got her niece there and they ran the house and everyone knew it. Years after, I had Dr Ferguson, who succeeded Dr Shaw, and I told him I used to live there till Mrs Wall came. "Oh," he said, "Mrs Wall!! I was locum in her time and I don't forget her. She was a Tartar!"

I believe poor Dr Shaw was made so uncomfortable and unhappy. He used to be out so much at night seeing patients and he took too much spirits. He was greatly loved by all the poor people. Dr Ferguson said many people missed Dr Shaw when he went away and spoke of him for years.

I went back to Mrs Newman after this. They wanted me so, the dear little Margery Alice had died suddenly of meningitis, and Olive and Hilda had been away with scarlet fever. Mrs Newman

82

went to fetch them home and told them there was a big surprise for them. They tried to guess and just as they neared home Olive guessed and she came running in and hugged me. They were pleased.

I had my 21st birthday the end of that year, but before that I had to go into the cottage hospital at Bromley to have an operation on my legs for the removal of some varicose veins.

I was happy to be back with them. Mrs Newman went to her home for a change some time after and I carried on. I think I was back with them for another year.

I used to go to my old Bible class, and one Sunday I was a little late and they were praying and another young girl, Alice, came into the porch. I spoke to her and made friends. Going home I asked her if she loved the Lord. She said her mother did and she wanted to, so she made her decision while we walked together and how glad her dear mother was when she wrote to tell her.

I went to see her and found she and another young girl from their village, Cranbrook, were engaged by this woman, the daughter of an elderly lady they knew, but this daughter was leading a strange life, supposed to be keeping a boarding house.

She was not fit to have two young country girls in her charge. I wrote to Alice's mother and she came up and took her away. Alice went to an elderly couple I knew in Bromley and stayed some time.

36. MOTHER IN MOURNING

I was very sorry when Mother wanted me to leave Mrs Newman and come home and poor Mrs Newman cried.

For the past three years Mother had withdrawn, like Queen Victoria mourning her beloved Albert. Mother was mourning my little brother Bertie, her darling. Bertie was never very strong and soon tired. He went to school for two years and then it was realized he had a heart defect, and Mother had to wrap him in shawls and let him lie on the sofa.

He was a merry but thoughtful little boy, never complaining and always concerned about others, asking: "Does your head ache Mother?" or "Are you very tired tonight Father?" The whole family used to talk and read to him and tell him stories.

When we were working away we could only see him in our time off. He could read and write quite well at six and amused himself, drawing little pictures and writing and reading to himself if Mother was busy.

Dropsy developed in his legs and body, and he said one day when he was eight: "Mother I'm truly sorry, but I don't think I shall live here long. I think Jesus wants me to go to heaven."

Once when I came home for the day and was putting my hat on getting ready to go back to the station, he said: "Don't go Alice." When I said I must, he said: "Well don't go the field way." "Why ever not?" I asked, laughing. "Because there is a great big 'cow jim pie ana' beetle in the field and he will spring out and eat you up." He was always inventing terrible beasties.

What he liked best was for Mother and any of us at home at the time to sit down and tell him about foreign places, and he used to say he would like to ride a camel and visit the Pyramids or go to the Great Wall of China. Then he would ask us to sing.

Bertie died that year, before his ninth birthday, and Mother could not bear it, and would shut herself in her bedroom every afternoon and lie on her bed as if all the purpose had gone out of her life. Father had regular employment when the hospitals were built and there was no need for Mother to go out to work as we girls were earning and as long as we had the necessities of life, luxuries never bothered us.

When I came home from the Newmans', Father told me the place was like a cold, dead house. I did all I could to make him comfortable and to rouse Mother, and in a measure succeeded. Mr Smith, a neighbour, said he had heard they wanted nurses at the new fever hospital in Tooting. I thought no more about it until my sister A came home and there was no peace, she was so domineering, so I applied at the hospital and was accepted.

It seems they had applied to Mrs Newman and asked if I was strong and she had to say I had had an operation on my legs. I liked the work but could not stay there many months as I again suffered with my legs, running up and down stairs, and up and down wards to attend the patients.

85

37. ROTTEN FRUIT THROWN IN CRANBROOK

I had been writing to Alice at Cranbrook and her mother invited me for a change. I went down and following her directions got into the little horse bus at Cranbrook station with the other passengers. The man who drove it said: "Oh I'll put you down Miss." It was dark and I wondered how far it was, as he kept putting people down till I was the last.

Eventually he stopped and a voice said: "Here you are dearie," and Alice's mother welcomed me and I found myself in a nice cottage and a hot meal prepared. Oh she was kind but that night I had such a bad turn of biliary colic, and was in pain and felt so cold and afraid to disturb anyone. There were only candles to light one to bed, and I tossed about in darkness.

But in the morning Mrs Evenden was so kind. My head ached terribly and she bathed it and put vinegar cloths on my forehead, I had never experienced such kindness.

At the weekend she told me about the work the Salvation Army were doing and asked me if I would like to go with her to the meeting. As there was no other evangelical work there, I went and soon was helping the two young officers, a captain and lieutenant. They did a lot of work and there were some wonderful conversions.

We used to have crowds at the open air meetings and often got rotten fruit thrown at us. I helped in the meetings and was so glad to find a place of service. Soon it was proposed I should become a candidate and I offered for slum work or abroad and looked forward to training.

When I went home Mother and Father were all against it but I went forward and when I got the form to fill up I felt overjoyed. I had so very little schooling but had tried to improve myself and hoped to be able to serve the Lord and was willing to go anywhere. So after filling up the form I had to take it to a doctor.

I went to a Christian doctor, but after some questions and examining me he said: "I can't fill this in. Now," said he, "sit down! Stand up! Sit down! Now stand up!" Then he sounded me and said: "You have had rheumatic fever." "Oh yes," I said, "when I was 14."

He said: "It doesn't matter when but your heart is affected and you could not do anything that would strain or tax it, you must live a quiet life if you want to live." So I had to give up all thought of it.

Nellie at Brentwood where she looked after children with ringworm

38. SOME LADIES DID NOT BEHAVE AS LADIES

I had to get a post. Mother suggested dressmaking as I was handy with my needle, so I went to a dressmaker who lived near by and had several apprentices. She tried me out and then engaged me as an improver. We had to take the finished work to the houses and see if everything was quite in order at the final fitting. Oh! how I had to work.

Braided trimmings, frogs, tucks and pleats were in vogue, as well as flounced and many gored skirts. Ladies favoured tight fitting bodices with dozens of tiny buttons, short and three quarter coats, and lacy, frilly blouses. Two and three petticoats were the rule.

Underwear was generally a chemise, a pair of corsets known as stays, and a camisole, which was made of cambric, tucked and lace edged and buttoned down the front. We wore long white drawers which were buttoned with a band at the waist.

Mother favoured Queen Victoria's style of drawers which my daughter later described as 'two legs on a string'. These were voluminous and wrapped round the waist and overlapped before being tied by waist tapes. These had to be checked that they were still attached after each laundering, to avoid disaster.

The youngest apprentices did a great deal of fetching and carrying and picking up pins off the carpet and threading needles. The dressmaker cut out the garments.

I often had to make the alterations and I did not mind going out to fit a customer but some ladies in those days did not behave as ladies, they were rude, critical and demanding, and often kept the account owing till they required something else. Then the husbands would pay up.

I could do the better work but the dressmaker was unable or unwilling to pay me. I was putting in long hours with no advance in wages.

It was nothing to start at 8 am and still be busy at 8 pm, working in poor light and with very little heat and only three quarters of an hour break. I was not getting enough fresh air and had eye strain so I decided to leave. I had been there for nearly two years.

David, Pat's son, about 1919

39. BICYCLES MADE FOR THREE

My sisters had acquired second hand bicycles and learnt to ride. They tried to teach me but I kept wobbling and falling off. Bicycles were much higher in those days and there was farther to fall.

They managed to get the same week's holiday and decided to go on a cycling tour, putting up for the night wherever they were when they felt they had had enough for the day. They were told to send a postcard or letter each day so my parents had some idea of where they were.

One day we received a letter from Ruth saying she had lost the other two at some cross roads, so she bought a pound of tomatoes, sat down by the roadside, 'nursed my secret sorrows' and ate the lot, and she wasn't quite sure where she was. Fortunately they all met up again before night.

Another day a bull got out of a field and came after them and they said they pedalled for dear life but it would have been much easier if they had not had to go up a slight hill.

My parents did not take a holiday that I can recall. They visited relatives by train or horse bus. Father liked to go on top in the bus and smoke but both these were considered a little daring for ladies to do.

At every steep hill some of the passengers got out and walked up to save the horses, which had to do so many miles and then be changed at inns or stables on the way. The ostlers led out the fresh animals and unhitched the tired ones and led them away to be fed and watered.

It was a pleasant way to travel if you did not mind the jolting and the rather hard seats. The bus steps were high and the ladies had to bunch their skirts and be helped up.

Mother once ventured to go on the Inner Circle to see a friend when the Underground was in use in London. When the train reached the place she wanted, she got up in a dignified manner after it had stopped and went to the door, slowly getting out backwards as was her custom.

A helpful porter pushed her back in as he thought she was getting on, and this happened twice more, so she had her money's worth, riding round the Inner Circle three times.

Then she gave it up, and moving a little quicker, got out at the station where she had first got on, and came home without having seen her friend. Father had a good laugh but Mother felt quite cross and told him it was no laughing matter. She could not think what the world was coming to, with the trains being so fast and the porters so pushing.

40. VISIT TO HARLESTON

An invitation came from Norfolk from Father's two unmarried sisters for us four girls to visit them. We had planned a holiday all together at Yarmouth and my sister Agnes had booked the rooms. The three others cycled there and I went by steamer. I met a nice couple named Benskin who told me where they were going to stay.

When I arrived, I discovered there was only one bedroom, with a small single bed and a double one. Ruth took the small bed, Aggie made Nellie sleep against the wall and I had to be on the outside but Aggie kept pushing me, and twice I fell out and landed with a bump on the floor.

Next day I met the Benskins and they told me there was a small spare room at their digs and took me round to see the landlady who agreed I could sleep there for a small sum.

We had to go on the Tuesday to Harleston to visit my aunts so we caught the train and found we had to walk over a mile from the station. At last we arrived and they gave us a royal welcome, with various Norfolk delicacies to eat, and took us to visit some cousins who lived in a pretty cottage and gave us tea.

We stayed chatting for a while and then said goodbye and walked leisurely down the lanes to catch the next train to Yarmouth. But we learnt there was only one train a day in each direction and we had missed the returning one. There was nothing for it but to walk back to the aunts'. Two of us were accommodated at Aunt Lizzie's and two went to Cousin Fanny.

When we woke in the morning the birds were singing and the fragrance from the roses at the little casement windows was wonderful. Seeing we had time to spend before the train was due, the aunts took us to see their old home.

We were impressed and wondered that Father could bear to leave it. There seemed no rush or hurry as if the village had not been disturbed for centuries, and the peace and charm had rubbed off on to the inhabitants.

I did not see the sea until I was grown up and could not understand what the noise was until I watched the waves advancing and retreating on the shingle. Of course I had to taste it and was surprised to find it so salt.

One day I hired a costume and a bathing machine from the woman attendant, went up the steps into the little wooden box and the horse drew me a few yards out into the ocean. I changed into my ankle and wrist length serge costume and gingerly went down the steps into the water, but hung on to the steps as I could not swim.

After bobbing up and down for a while I went back into the bathing machine and dressed and then called to the woman, who led the horse back and hitched him up to take me to the beach.

My sister Ruth had gone to be nurse at the new Epsom Asylum. I tried two fever hospitals but the doctors would not pass me. When I heard how they were taking on a large number of nursing staff at the asylum and you did not have to have a medical examination for three months, I applied with my references and was engaged.

I arrived about 4 o'clock, the patients' tea time, and was sent to a ward as soon as I had taken off my outdoor clothes and was given a cap and apron and asked to help. I was very scared of the patients, but determined to stay a year if possible.

When Ruth heard I was there she came to my bedroom and said: "What did you come here for? You won't stop a month." I said: "I will if I keep well," and I did stay a little over the year.

At first I slept in a room next to the ward, with a small curtained window looking into it, and when I went to bed I fastened my door very securely as I did not feel safe.

One patient named Dora sat most of the day copying out proverbs on pieces of paper. She had been a school mistress and seemed quiet enough. But she had a reluctance to getting dressed in the morning and would pull the sheets up over her. When I stooped down to try and get her out I had a piece of paper waved in my face with 'Kind hearts are more than coronets' written on it. It was disconcerting.

Two or three weeks passed and as nothing happened I wondered if she was there by mistake. But that very lunch time she suddenly got up and rammed her basin of rice pudding down on a nurse's head. Shortly after she attacked another nurse in a corner and tried to pull her hair out. When I went to the rescue, Dora shouted: "Keep away, little Nurse Green, I don't want to hurt you."

94

Dulcibel was a vicar's wife and had good manners and refined speech. The first day she saw me she welcomed me like her long lost friend and called me 'my dearest Emma'. Thinking it best to agree with her to keep the peace, I allowed myself to be called Emma for several days.

Then one evening when I came on duty she suddenly charged towards me shouting: "Emma, you vile trollop, you are the bitch who took my husband from me. I'm going to do for you."

I fled and the Sister kindly shoved me into the linen room and said: "Stay there." She sent Dulcibel to bed, telling her Emma was not within a mile of the place. Next day I was Nurse Green again, and the Sister gave me a lesson as to when it was best to humour patients and when to deal firmly with them.

Magda was a nymphomaniac. I had never met one before. Sister told me the German woman had to be closely watched whenever a man came into the ward, whether it was a workman or a doctor, as she had been known to strip one like lightning.

The day came when the piano tuner called. Magda was locked in the nearest bathroom and I was left outside to guard her. She was furious and kept shouting at me. Then, quite unknown to us, the window cleaners arrived outside and I thought she would smash the bathroom window.

I sent the piano tuner for help, as it happened just when the other patients had been taken for exercise. She went wild and smashed everything in reach, so she had to go into the padded cell to cool off.

Many of the patients were not violent but stood about like zombies, sometimes standing naked by their beds. Another thought she was a dog and went about on all fours, barking, and would only respond to Fido.

When her husband came to see her he always looked so sad, as he had three children at home and he kept hoping she would get better and return to them.

It was sad to see even little girls there. One aged 12 had deliberately put her baby sister in the path of an oncoming tram and watched with glee when the baby was run over.

Len and Bertha, about 1912

42. SHIRLEY SCHOOLS

Before I left the asylum I had some bad fainting turns. Very early one morning I wanted to go to the toilet and put on my dressing gown, took my keys and fastened my door. Every door had to be unlocked and locked as you passed through.

I must have unlocked the other door and locked it behind me and then fallen in the stone passage way. When I came round I was cold and for a moment could not remember where I was.

Feeling stone floor and stone wall and being in the dark, I thought I was buried till my hand touched the bunch of keys. I got up and felt my way to the door, opened it and managed a few steps as far as the head nurse's door. She must have heard me try to knock and touch the handle of her door for she opened it and I fell in on to her, so she put me on her bed.

Later the doctor saw me and said I must leave. I told him I had resigned, but I had filled in a form of application for a post as nurse at the children's infirmary at Shirley Schools,[10] near Croydon, a complex of cottages for poor children, with a school, church and hospital.

I was at home in between the two posts for two weeks and my sister Aggie came home from Devonport after her engagement was broken off. She had been there over three years helping in an orphanage, so she said she would be able to get a post sooner than I but it did not happen that way and she was home

---

[10] Built for Bermondsey Board of Guardians. Grouped cottage homes were a Poor Law institution and resulted from a policy of removing children from workhouses. There were also scattered homes where a small number of children lived in ordinary houses, such as the Hanwell house where later Nellie was in charge. - Editor.

three months, and what a trial she was to Mother and to me when I went home for my half day.

One day as I went out of the main gate I saw a notice, they wanted temporary assistant mothers for some of the cottages. When I went home Mother said: "If she doesn't get a post she will drive me mad."

I did not want her at Shirley but I felt it was right to give her the chance and I spoke to the headmaster. He said: "Oh send for her." She came, and he came up to the infirmary to see her.

She proffered her testimonials but he waved them away and said Nurse Green is enough testimonial. So she came and was sent to a boys' cottage. She could manage the boys, she ran them like an army sergeant major, and when the permanent posts were advertised she filled in a form of application and went before the board and was appointed, though younger than usual, because Mr R said she was quite capable.

At the children's infirmary we were three nurses and three domestic staff. I was the last nurse, the second was leaving and the nurse in charge was going on holiday. She went, and got married so they both left and I had to run the wards alone.

They sent for a nurse who had been in their employ but she was so nervous on night duty that the doctor said she had better help me in the day work and we could share the night treatments as there were no serious cases.

But Nurse Phillips could never wake until called in the morning so it meant my getting up at 2 am and 6 am. I carried on for some time, like this, not getting my time off.

When they sent the trained nurse up from the probationary wards, I should have gone on night duty and have left Nurse Phillips to work with her, but as I knew all about the outpatients and the dispensing I had to show her all the routine. At that time we were without a dispenser and no one else had any experience.

When I asked her to sign my off duty pass she would let it slip and I was upset as I had a lot of time owing to me. When she knew the work she was very nasty, so I resigned.

At first they refused to take my resignation, gave me some time off and asked me to come back on night duty. I did this but it did not work out. The new nurse left for me all the chores she should have done before going off duty. Then in the mornings she would come on late to relieve me and expect me to have done some of her work. Things got worse and eventually I did leave.

Tooting Broadway 1912-14, looking southwards towards Merton with Defoe Road (now Garratt Lane) on the right and Mitcham Road on the left. Picture courtesy of Wandsworth Local History Library

I stayed at home for a few months as Mother wanted me to be with her. Father also was pleased to see me and said: "Now we shall have one of Alice's nice meat puddings. Mother, you always make yours too dry."

I did some dressmaking but it was only enough to pay my board and lodging, and ladies who came in carriages expected you to take the finished garments to them, which often meant walking three or four miles. They never offered fare or refreshment.

One evening I had been to Balham to take a blouse I had made for a customer and on walking back I stopped at the old tram depot as Gypsy Smith had a mission there. I had heard he was a famous Gypsy evangelist.

I think most of the people were in. A young man stood at the entrance giving away Christian literature and I asked him if the place was very crowded as I wanted to bring Mother one evening. I think it was a fortnight's mission. He told me the best night to bring her, and went on to talk of mission.

He asked me if I had been to the Torrey and Alexander mission at Albert Hall, two years previously. I had, and then he told me he was in the choir there. We talked for some time and then I said I must get a tram home. He came to the stop and saw me on the tram. The next evening I went to the evening service and he walked with me to the tram again.

He asked me if I would like some of the magazines and to my surprise came to our house with them after the meeting. After seeing me several times, and I had taken my mother and sister Nellie to hear Gypsy Smith and introduced them, he came to visit very often and spent some time with me.

He told me he loved me and I was soon very fond of him. I had never flirted or had anything to do with young men. Mother was very strict so we were all very shy and when he showed me such attention, bringing me roses etc, it was very sweet.

I had to get another post as the needlework did not pay. I made a few applications and was selected. I chose one in London to be near him, as he was in Fleet Street. So I was appointed nurse to St Giles' Infirmary (and Workhouse), Endell Street, W.C. I went there the beginning of December 1905 and all my off duty time was spent with him.

We used to walk in Hyde Park in the evenings, and if I was off duty in the day time we would go on the Serpentine, he taught me to row as he had been to sea for some years.

Although he came home with me often I had not seen anyone belonging to him. He just said he had a sister in law at Gravesend, and though he gave me presents, he did not give me a ring in spite of our being engaged. He said only the wedding ring was important. I believed him and trusted him completely.

He did ask me if he went abroad and got a post if I would go out to him and be married. Living abroad did not appeal to me and I said I would want to be married at home and I was sure Mother would not agree to it.

Sometimes he was away for his firm as he was the advertising manager and I used to receive frequent picture postcards and letters from him.

We went on like this for a year and seven months, from September 1905 to April 1907. Then he was away and I did not hear from him. Just then I was very poorly over some teeth extractions and had to be off duty a few days. I could not sleep for pain. One night I dozed off and dreamt I had a letter from him and was reading it, when I came to the words 'I can never marry you'.

When my friend came in, Nurse Byers, to see how I was, I told her my dream. "Oh," she said, "I expect you will get two or three letters to make up and everything will be alright. You know dreams come in reverses." After her breakfast she came up with two letters and one was from him. I had not read far when I came to those words, that I had seen in my dream.

In the early days when he came to see or call for me at home, Mother said she would see him first one evening. It seems she asked him about his relations and if he was single or a widower. When she came out of the parlour she said I could go in. He was quite vexed she should have doubted him and so I was deceived. I believed him when he said he was single.

It was a great shock and made me quite ill. He wrote to say he could not marry me but would come to see me and tell me all, and asked for my forgiveness. Also he would write to Mother so she would know.

When he came to tell me the reason for his letter, he admitted he was a married man with three children and some of his trips away were time spent at home with his wife and family. He said he was trying to get a divorce though he knew I would not marry a divorced man.

I had no sympathy from my home folk and was very unhappy. Mother rated me as if I had brought disgrace to the family by not seeing through him. After some months my health suffered as I was afraid to go out because it upset me to see him, yet he was always hanging about hoping to see me, so I stayed in my room on my off duty.

44. MARRIAGE

A new officer came to St Giles'. I heard the nurses and other staff talking of him saying he was a fine man. I was then in charge of the men's ward and when any man in the workhouse complained of illness, this officer had to bring them up to my ward to see the doctor. If any belonging to another parish were ill, they had to be sent back to their own parish, by horse ambulance.

There were two one morning, and I explained to him what he had to do in regard to them, but when I crossed the court to go to my dinner, a man said the new officer is looking for you. I had to explain all over again about the men's cards and transfer. I thought he was obtuse but he told me afterwards it was an excuse to talk to me again.

One evening I went out for a few minutes to buy something for one of the nurses and took it up to the men's ward where she was on night duty. When I heard Mr M call me I stopped on the stairs and he came up a few steps to speak to me, remarking that I did not go out much and ending by asking me to go out for a walk the next evening, saying it would do me good.

Suddenly I thought it would be the best thing to do, as Mr G would then see this fine big man with me and stop coming round about and pestering me.

So our courtship began, though I never dreamt it at the time. Then I saw much of him in his work and saw that he was thorough and conscientious, with a great sense of humour. He was a Dublin man and had so many witty Irish sayings he could keep you amused, especially as he had an infectious laugh and, except when he was roused, a twinkle in his blue eyes.

He was older than me, there were 10 years between us, and a Roman Catholic. He was reassured when he asked the infirmary Catholic chaplain about me. I had got to know the chaplain quite well and he described me as being as pure as a nun.

We used to go out. I went to the Wesleyan Chapel, and he used to meet me afterwards. He used to have his day off and promised one Sunday to come back and meet me, but did not come. This nearly caused me to break with him, but he promised it would not happen again.

He had been to his sister in law's. As this was the same thing Mr G had told me, I thought I must ask him more about his relations. He was a widower, but when I asked him if he had any children he said: "a boy." Then one day I asked if he was the only child, he said he had two.

I said: "Now if you have any more tell me. I cannot go home each week and say another child." Then he told me he had been a widower seven years and was left with four[11] children. The baby died soon after her mother and the little girl died of meningitis at the age of 10 only the Christmas before he met me.

I took him home to see my people and he took me one evening to Bow to see his sister in law who was looking after his boys. I knew she did not like me but I saw David fourteen,[12] and Jim eight.

I became engaged to him 3 January 1908 and he bought my ring. I chose what was known as a 'keeper' of 18 carat gold with fern leaves and ivy engraved on it. He also bought the wedding ring, a broad band of 22 carat gold.

---

[11] He had also had a baby girl who was buried in Malta where he was serving with the army. - BM.

[12] David was born in 1892 and Jim in 1900, so David must have been older than 14 and Jim not quite eight. - BM.

I had been at St Giles' for two and a half years and this was his first Poor Law post after leaving the army. We thought we would get a joint appointment and though we filled up several application forms, did not get selected. I thought it was because we were not married, as the couples chosen seemed to be all married.

We decided I would leave and do some private nursing after we were married, he would stay on so as to get his testimonial.[13]

He was due for holiday in May, so we were married on 2 May 1908 and I had made the arrangements to go to Brighton for our honeymoon. Neither of us would get married in the other's place of worship so we decided on a register office.

I made my wedding dress of turquoise blue pique. It had a skirt with 16 gores, a fitted bodice and a white silk blouse. I wore a white straw hat and carried a small bunch of lilies of the valley.

Beside our family I had two friends, Alice from Cranbrook and Minnie Watts, another nurse at St Giles', and afterwards we all went home to roast sirloin of beef, Yorkshire pudding and vegetables from the garden, and a favourite coconut castle pudding and cake.

It was a lovely day but very warm. I changed into a green costume and we went to Balham station. I had got the tickets and been told the platform. We went up the stairs, but the porter told us another platform. It was very hot but P got very vexed at having to carry our luggage up and down stairs.

---

[13] I think it was a year to get a reference. Alice had one such testimonial signed by the hospital authorities regarding her work, conduct and general ability. - BM.

He was so cross by the time the train came in, so we sat in silence all the way to Brighton. I did try to draw his attention to the spring flowers but got no response. I thought, what a wedding day! Well I had to get used to a quick Irish temper. It took a long time.

Len's class at Broadwater Road School, Tooting. Len is on the second right of the back row

When we reached Brighton and went out of the station many boys offered to carry our luggage but he would not let them, and I knew it was quite a walk.

We arrived at last and went up to our bed sitting room. It had been booked by me in my married name owing to the various pranks played on newly weds, an apple pie bed etc.

The landlady was middle aged and kindly, a widow, who settled us in and gave us some tea (we also had use of the downstairs dining room), then asked how long we had been married. I said it was some time and she was quite satisfied, for we certainly did not appear like newly weds. My new husband was only just beginning to thaw.

After unpacking we went for a walk, I was very tired. We had a thunderstorm in the night and it cooled the air. After breakfast we went for a lovely walk, it was beautiful after the rain.

Once, before my marriage, I had been sitting on the sofa at home beside Pat when Mother came into the room and called me into the kitchen. "There is no need to sit so close to the man, even if you are going to marry him," she said. "You should sit on a chair on the other side of the room. Sitting beside men puts ideas into their heads."

I went back and made some excuse, not saying anything of what Mother wanted me for as I knew he would resent it, he never took any liberties with me. Now we were married and away from home I felt more free, but quite shy.

To make matters worse, the double bed had a well worn spring mattress. My husband weighed 17 stone (108.2 kg) and I weighed eight. Most of the first night was spent by me hanging on to the side of the bed, as his weight made him sink into the middle and every time I let go I rolled down on top of him. After a few grunts on his part, as he was generally a heavy sleeper, we began to giggle. We realized we should have to adjust the bed somehow, without offending the landlady. Next morning we tried propping up the middle but then we both rolled off. In the end we used to put the bolster down between us before we settled for the night.

It turned cold and mother sent me my fur to wear, especially when we were on the front. We arranged to view the ships one afternoon as P wanted to show me over, but a thick mist came down and we could not see anything.

Another day we went for a ride in a brake and had a good view of the downs from the top of the horse drawn vehicle. It was a bit windy, so I had to tie my hat on with a scarf.

Pat was smoking a cigarette, but I did not like them and when the brake returned I went into a shop and bought him his first pipe. That evening we had a lot of fun as he tried it out.

We decided to leave Brighton a day earlier than we had planned as there was a cheap fare on offer and then we could have a day in our own rooms. I had furnished a bed sitting room at Mother's, expecting it to be only a temporary arrangement until we could get a joint post.

In the morning when we woke P offered to go down and make a cup of tea, he wanted to do it for me but soon came back to say Mother would not let him. Later she scolded me for letting him attempt it, she said it was my place to wait on him.

He had to return to St Giles' as it was a living in post and I stayed at home, only seeing him on his off duty.

My sister Ruth had married a very delicate young man who was soon found to be suffering from tuberculosis. Her baby (Kathleen) was born on 3 January 1908 and with her husband ill she went back to nursing, part time, at St Mary Abbot's Hospital in Kensington.

I used to go over and look after the baby and stay the night. She was the most fretful baby I ever handled, grizzling all night, and her mother had no patience with her.

Then one day Mother went to Wimbledon to see Mrs Hampton. She had been very poorly for a long time and her doctor advised an operation. She was to have it at home and her husband, Colonel Hampton, had asked Sir James Cantlie to do it. (He was not Sir then but later, in 1918.) Mrs Hampton wanted me to nurse her, so I went over to care for her.

Her doctor came to assist and brought along a district nurse just for the operation but after that I nursed her and *how* grateful she was. She was such a good patient and the surgeon praised her, and also told me he thought me a very good nurse. He was so nice.

One morning when her husband brought us a cup of tea she asked him to speak a word for Pat to get his name forward on the War Office list, or try to get him something else, so we could be together.

Colonel Hampton said he would like to see him and his army papers. I wrote to him and he came, I suppose he was nervous and that upset his temper. After seeing Colonel Hampton, Mrs

Hampton suggested we went for a walk and her daughters sat with her.

We walked across Wimbledon Common but P was very cross and it was not a very happy walk. I was glad to get back and Mrs H knew I had been upset.

She was so kind and understanding, and she had a great sense of humour, which was necessary as the colonel was peppery. While she was being given chloroform for the operation, Sir James asked: "Madam, do you feel drunk?" "No, sir, do you?" was her response.

She was sorry to part with me when I had to leave. She said she had never been nursed so well. They gave me a breakfast set and Mrs H two lovely old terracotta jugs. I've had them now 54 years and they were her mother's.

47. PREGNANT

After this, I was asked to do holiday duty at Shirley Schools, where I had been at the children's infirmary. I went to the probation villa for children just admitted. I had 30, 15 boys and 15 girls. Every three weeks fresh ones came and the others were sent to the permanent villas. Boys and girls were kept separate till they were 14 and then they were placed in living in jobs.

I found the children's clothes in the storeroom very much in need of repair. I set to work to get all in order with two girls to help sew on buttons and tapes etc, while I did the more difficult work. The villa was purpose built and quite pleasant to work in. There was a nice little cook and a housemaid and they did their work well.

But no one seemed to be concerned about repairs. Curtains had hems hanging down, some chairs were rickety, and rugs and carpets were frayed.

I had only been there about two weeks when I had an accident. I went to the door with the doctor to see him out and when I turned back caught my foot in the loose binding of the big doormat. I tried to save myself from falling and took two strides and slid along to the other end of the hall and fell against the wall. I felt something go in the groin.

As it was Saturday we had planned to take the children to Shirley Hills for a picnic. It was the first time they had seen the countryside. I found the walk very trying and when I went to bed, found I had ruptured myself. The next day was my day off and my husband was to meet me at East Croydon station and we were going to spend the day at home.

It was very trying walking over two miles to East Croydon and I had to get a taxi back at night. Matron at the infirmary said I must tell the doctor when he came next. He examined me and said: "You will have to have an operation." I had an inguinal hernia.

I told him I was pregnant and he said: "In that case you had better be fitted with a special truss." I went up to London and was measured for a truss. This was a support, but it only put off the time when I should have the operation.

I did duty for three months at Shirley and then went home. I did some dressmaking and also had Ruth's Kathleen to care for.

After her husband died and she went back to full time work she asked me to take the baby, as she could not get anyone to keep her very long she was so fractious. I was glad when her father's maiden aunts in Kent offered to take her. They kept her for 13 years and spoilt her.

I had to earn money as I was not receiving any from Pat, he was paying his sister in law for the two boys' keep. David was a Post Office messenger boy and I had asked P to let me have them.

One day he had been to see them and David had begged his father to sign a paper for him to enter the Royal Field Artillery. He did. Jim was at school. He took after his mother and had black hair and grey eyes, but David was fair haired and had the blue eyes of his father.

P agreed that I should have Jim, after the baby was born. In the kitchenette adjoining the bed sitting room I put up a little bed for Jim, everything was ready for him.

48. MOTHERHOOD AND STEPMOTHERHOOD

My baby was born on 5 April 1909 after a terribly hard labour of 24 hours and having to have a removal by forceps and two doctors, I had haemorrhaged very badly. It was a miracle I came through. Lennie weighed over 11 lbs.

How many severe illnesses the Lord has brought me through, how much we have to praise Him for.

P had left St Giles' and went to Mitcham Workhouse as assistant master. It was still a living in post, but nearer Tooting. After that he got a War Office job, working for the chaplain to the forces. He brought Jim home when the baby was only a week old, he did not realize how ill I was.

Mrs Woodley who was nursing me lived two doors away and kindly took Jim to play with her children and Mother gave him his meals downstairs. He was very naughty and stayed out playing long after he was told to come in. When he did Mother made him wash, and sent him up to bed.

He came into my room and sat down. I said: "Undress quickly and go to bed, Jim." He said: "No I will stay here." I had a tiny lamp burning, and could see his bed from my room, but he would not go. At last I said: "Well you will have to sit in the dark," so he went after all.

But in the middle of the night he began to scream. I called to him to ask if he was in pain, he would not answer but continued to scream. At last I got out of bed, I was not supposed to for another 10 days and well I knew it as I had a prolapse through doing so.

When I went to him I pulled the bedclothes down from over his head. He said he was afraid the nurses from the hospital at the back might climb over our wall, at the bottom of the garden. This was impossible he knew, as the wall was very high.

I learnt later that his aunt had filled his head with the notion that all stepmothers were hateful so he had determined to play me up and do nothing he was told. A neighbour took him to school, and I began to get about but my baby did not get on.

He was such a big baby when born, but I had no strength to feed him and soon had to try bottle feeding. Nothing seemed to suit him and he lost weight and cried continually. Often I got up in the night and walked about with him, so as not to wake his father.

One day P said would Horlicks Malted Milk suit him, as they had been advised to try it for Jim. I went to our old chemist for the usual lime (gripe) water ordered by the doctor, and I asked him if Horlicks Malted Milk was suitable for young babies. He put his glasses on and read the directions, and told me it was so.

I bought the first bottle. It was not known much, and I had never heard of it. I took it home and made a bottle according to directions and Lennie kept it down and went to sleep. From then on he grew and was a normal happy baby.

When he was nearly three months, David was to come home on leave. I had only seen him once before I married. I made him a nice fruit cake for his birthday, and gave him a welcome, but oh dear, they had both been set against me by their aunt, and their father had no control over them.

After we had gone to bed one night, P said to me: "I think David is reading in bed with a candle." I said: "Why did you not stop him?" so he called out: "Your mother does not like you to read in bed with a candle," which was no help.

114

I think he was at home for two weeks that time, but all the years and through the 1914 war, sometimes a month's leave, he never offered me anything for his keep, though he must have received money for it.[14]

Jim never offered anything either, even when he was receiving pay. I did my best for them.

Pat, Aggie and Alice (right) with Bob the dog

---

[14] The army allowed cash to cover leave expenses. - BM.

In 1910 I was expecting my next baby and I found it tiring work carrying little Lennie up and down stairs to answer the door and do errands or hang out washing. I heard of a downstairs flat to rent farther down the road, at number 53, and took it. It was only a few doors from my parents'.

I managed to move most of our things with the pram, and Dad and P brought the chest of drawers and bed springs, big box etc in a barrow. That was in October and my baby was due in December. I got things straight and it was much more convenient.

One afternoon Jim came back from school and said he had been sent home because he had swallowed a marble. I said: "Well now, you must drink a lot of salt water and if that does not do, a dose of castor oil." He made a great fuss, but as there was no sign of a marble, I think it was an excuse to stay away from school.

Christmas came and as I expected baby just then, I bought a leg of pork for our Christmas dinner so that there would be something to cut for a few days. I managed to cook it and the pudding and some mince pies. We had the same cold the next day, but all day I was having pains.

In the evening Mother came and we sat talking, I did not want to tell her I was having pains and thought it might be a long time as before. So when she said goodnight I told Pat and we put a match to the fire in the bedroom and I put the baby clothes ready.

Mother came back again with some ginger wine and we had to let her know. Then I told P I would undress and he had better go for Mrs Potts who was going to nurse me.

116

When he came back with Mrs Potts, she said: "You had better take the cot mattress out and the little one." He made Lennie comfortable in a corner of the kitchen and then she sent him for the doctor, I had engaged Dr Ferguson. When he came back it was with a doctor I did not know.

The doctor looked more like an artist. He wore a black velvet coat and a floppy black tie and his hair was curling on his shoulders. He sat by the fire and time went on. I had strong pains but after a while he said: "Why are you so nervous and trembling?" Mrs Potts said: "Oh she had a very bad time and haemorrhage when her boy was born." "Oh," he said and got instruments ready. I begged him not to use them.

They were with me all night, but what a good doctor he was, how he helped and though such a big baby[15] he managed without using the instruments. He would not let the midwife wash me but did it himself. He said he would have to put stitches in but I begged him not to and he said he would come back in case of haemorrhage.

When he came about 9 am he said he had had two more babies in the four hours after he left me, but not long labours like mine. My doctor, Dr Ferguson, had to go to Edinburgh as his mother was dying. When he came back he told me that the doctor who delivered my baby was a Dr John Morgan. Years later he told me John Morgan had a great sorrow and drank himself to death.

Bertha was born on Tuesday, 27 December 1910. Beforehand I had bought a second fireguard because there would be two open fires. On the following Sunday, Pat was cooking the dinner and Mother had just come in to see me and the baby. Mrs Potts had gone home. It seems Pat took the guard away from the fire while he opened the oven beside it. I used to just pull it forward.

---

[15] Not a big baby, but a shoulder presentation. - BM.

117

Little Lennie was running about and went forward with his little hands on the hot bars of the grate. He screamed and ran to me and climbed on to my bed. Mother picked up the baby and I told P where to get some white rags and carron oil. I covered his poor little hands with oil and wrapped them up and cuddled him and he cried himself to sleep. His hands healed without a scar.

I had his high chair put beside my bed and he sat in it each day after Mrs Potts had attended to me and the baby, and I would talk to him to amuse him. He was so good through it all.

The baby made feeding her a painful business as she was born with two bottom teeth. I told the doctor. "Oh no," he said, but took her to the window and it was confirmed. He said: "They will probably drop out soon," but they did not. It seems I cut my first tooth at four months old.

At this time Lennie was dressed in a frock and had long curls, as was the fashion with little boys. Many were not breeched until they were four but I decided to put him in little pants on his second birthday. So many people took him for a little girl.

This was partly because Mother had made him a doll out of old black woollen stockings stuffed with rags. It had a pair of trousers with a red stripe down the side like a postman, and also a purple dress, so that it could be of either sex. It was called Jack when it was a boy and Violet when it was a girl.

118

When baby Bertha was six months we had to move for Mother to live with us.

Mother and Father had been married 35 years and were growing apart. Mother had become rather introverted after Bertie's death, and Father was always quiet and did not realize how she felt. But my sister Agnes persuaded Mother to leave Father. She told me I should have to take Mother to live me with and get a house to take us all.

Pat did not like the idea but Mother was always very gracious to him so he accepted it. We moved down the road to a house in Cranmer Terrace. There was only a small garden but a recreation ground beyond.

My sister Nellie was ill, she had a weak heart, and I had to go up in the evening to see her in hospital while Mother and P took care of baby. Little Lennie would sleep, but baby was very much awake.

Later Nellie came home and she slept with Mother. During that time I tried to wean Bertha. She was 12 months and was walking about quite strongly. I had a lot of trouble to get rid of the milk and fainted several times one morning.

Another day I was hanging out the washing, Nellie had gone to another post, and baby Bertha missed her and got up the stairs. Mother called out of the window for me to come up gently behind her, she was afraid to look at her in case she fell. Bertha was nearly at the top and I got behind her. She looked into Mother's room and said: "Arnie," she thought her auntie would be there.

119

That summer there was an epidemic of diarrhoea and many deaths. Mother was the first to be prostrated with it and then baby and then I had it and hardly knew how to keep about.

We had to move. We did not know the houses had been built of old bricks and material from demolished slums and were infested with bugs. When the warm weather came and the house next door was redecorated they came into us, I could not cope with them.

When we saw an house in Fountain Road empty, I enquired and was told to apply to a shop in Putney. I went over to see the owner, an elderly man, and obtained the key on condition I went in that week, as he did not mean to lose a week's rent. It was much in need of repair, but we moved in and I had to pay the other landlord a week's rent in lieu of notice.

We had a few lively nights with mice, and Mother's big black cat Boof chasing and killing them. The first morning Mother came into my bedroom saying she could not stay in this house, the mice kept her awake. As if we could move again. That night her cat chased one into Pat's slipper and there was a slipper sliding over the floor with a mouse in the toe and a cat with his head in the slipper. Well he cleared the mice.

120

51. YEAR OF TROUBLE

We were only in that house one year, a year of trouble. First I was ill with pains in my abdomen and the doctor did not know what it was, but after some days in bed and hot fomentations[16] the pain went. I carried on for a few weeks, then it came on very suddenly. I had started my washing and only managed to get up the stairs, leaving half the washing done.

Mother called Mrs Payne next door and when Jim came in from school sent him for a doctor, not the one I had before. He gave me some little tablets for the pain, and it went on for days. I felt so ill and did not want any food. I was getting weaker and when the tablets were finished the pain was so bad. The doctor came in and looked at me.

Suddenly he opened the window and called his coachman to get an ambulance quickly, then he turned to me and said: "I think it's appendicitis." I was put in the ambulance and poor Pat came round the corner just in time to see it going. There were the three children, and Mother unable to get about. Little Bertha was a year and 11 months and Lennie three years and 8 months and Jim twelve.

I was very thin and they asked me many questions, and I expected them to operate but after the first day had rectal feeding and when the pain had subsided and Pat came to see me, he did not know what to do without me and asked the doctor if I could come home for Christmas. The doctor agreed but said if the pain returns you must send for the ambulance and come in for the operation.

---

[16] Lint soaked in very hot water and applied continually as a dressing to alleviate pain and reduce inflammation. - BM.

I was home through Christmas and on New Year's eve the pain returned. I had gone to bed early and Pat was reading to me when I felt it but did not tell him as I felt he must have a night's rest.

I was expecting Mother's old cousin Emma, as she had written to say she needed somewhere to stay for a time as the house in Dorset where she lived as housekeeper to a retired farmer was going under alterations.

In the morning I told Pat I would have to go back to hospital. At that time he was at the War Office. The day wore on. I had written out all I could think of as a guide for Emma, and it was getting dark when she arrived, carrying a birdcage in one hand and a carpetbag in the other.

She said she had walked from Waterloo, nearly seven miles from us, as the bird, a canary, did not like the train and certainly would not want to go on a tram.

Mother had her cat, so she told her they must fix the cage up in a safe place out of the cat's reach, and that took time. I was upstairs in bed and waiting to send Jim with the doctor's note for the ambulance, which I did as soon as I had seen Emma.

I had ordered a ton of coal, which arrived with the ambulance, so I was carried out and the coal in, and Emma talked to her bird.

Emma was Mother's Uncle Jesse's daughter. She was short and slight with a beaky nose and dark eyes, and she always wore a black blouse and skirt, and underneath a black and white striped petticoat with a pocket in which she kept her purse. She used to pull up her skirt to get money out, to everyone's embarrassment. She walked everywhere and time was of no consequence to her.

122

It was distressing leaving my little ones. This was Friday night and I had both operations done on the Monday morning, one for hernia and the other appendicectomy. I was in for a month.

A few months later, as little Bertha used to go upstairs and follow Lennie and had several falls, I took him to school, he had passed his fourth birthday. He went to the convent school near by. The children were quieter there than at the council school and were well supervised by the nuns, especially in the playground. My neighbour's husband, a gravedigger, used to bring him home at dinner time.

Lennie always stopped behind to kiss the nuns. He was sorry for all women without husbands, single or widows.

Len and Bertha at 82 Defoe Road in 1921. The photo taken by Pat's son David

52. WE THOUGHT HE WAS GONE

The end of July we were going over to see my sister Nellie in Greenford Avenue, Hanwell, where she was in charge of a girls' home and had the care of several girls. In one of her earlier posts she had worked at a children's home in Brentwood, Essex, looking after children who had ringworm.

It was a nice day but Lennie was feverish and I could not go so Pat took little Bertha and I sent for the doctor. He said: "Oh it's only a cold. He will soon be alright." But he was restless and more feverish. I took his temperature and charted it four hourly. I sent for the doctor again and he said: "What's wrong now?" I said: "I believe he has pneumonia."

He said: "What do you know about it?" I said: "I've nursed a good many cases and this is his temperature chart. Will you please sound him." He did and admitted it was pneumonia but did not seem too concerned. In a few days he had pleurisy too and I was poulticing him. We used to use linseed for poultices and they were heavy and smelly.

He was getting worse and we thought he was gone one night and the next day when the doctor came, he said he thought perhaps he had better go to hospital for an operation to remove the fluid. So when P came home we talked it over, as the doctor said if it was not too late, which was his fault. We sent for the ambulance and we went with him to hospital.

I was told to be there early the next morning, I went and they were just going to operate. When I went back in the afternoon he looked very bad and I was unable to rest or think, and I gave Jim and little Bertha their meals and cooked for Pat.

Each day I went up and down to the hospital, and then he was moved out on the balcony, this was the second week. So on the Sunday afternoon we went together and I said to Pat: "We shall see his bed when we get round the corner," but it was not there and when I reached the corridor a nurse said: "Sister wants to speak to you." She told me he would have to have another operation and have a piece of rib taken away. This was done the next day.

After a few weeks, when he was very ill, I was able to bring him home. He had bronchitis, for I think they had given him a bath just before he came out. We had a very restless night with him and he needed a lot of care.

When he was better I was advised to take him to the sea so I wrote to Mrs Lack, at whose house in Brighton we had stayed on our honeymoon, to ask if she could take us. She could, so I took the two children down.

I hired a goat cart for them as I could not expect them to walk much. They loved the goat and were very amused when it began eating some tamarisk I had picked and put in my string bag.

After I came back I looked about for somewhere else to live, as we had all been ill in the Fountain Road house. There was no damp course, it was damp and the floor boards were rotten and gave way at times.

We found an upstairs flat in Garratt Lane not far away and moved in. We had much more room, a big kitchen, living room, scullery, a sitting room, and a big room for Mother with windows looking out on the road and two large bedrooms above, and a toilet. She left her cat Boof with two neighbours who were very fond of him, the flat was unsuitable for a cat, and he lived to be 18.

We were there when war broke out in August 1914. We had taken the children to Southend and one morning Pat was reading his paper, when he said: "We shall have to go home as I must go back to the War Office. They will want us all." We cut short our holiday and took the children home.

The next day Pat went back to the War Office and he did not come home all night, and the next afternoon the bell rang and when I answered it, a stranger said: "Oh Mrs Mullen, your husband won't be home tonight and I don't know when he will as we are having to work and get some sleep when we can, and this is his pay as you will be wanting it. I'm Captain Day and I live in Tooting."

From then on Pat had to be at the War Office nights and days, I could never be sure when he would be home.

Jim had been a tremendous trouble. He had had a very different upbringing with his aunt. He was supposed to go to the Catholic church but unless his father went with him he would go off playing

126

and come back filthy dirty. He could say any amount of prayers but did not mean what he said.

He hated school and was always playing truant and got behind in his lessons and did not pick up until he went into the army on boy service (in effect an apprentice soldier) when he had to attend school. He could not be trusted to go on the simplest errand as he never brought back the right things or the right change.

Then there was an opening for a messenger boy at the War Office, and Pat took Jim up and secured the post for him. He used to go up by tram and came home every day but the times varied slightly.

One Sunday Pat was home for the day. When he went back he heard that Jim and another boy had been meddling with Lord Kitchener's[17] lift and got it out of order.

When Pat was home and Jim at the same time he gave him a good talking to, and on the next Sunday he called Jim to get up and went on with his own breakfast, but Jim did not appear and he was not in his bedroom.

We did not know for two days that he had not been to the War Office. Pat was up there so much and I had the two little ones to care for and it was so difficult shopping as things had not been rationed.

I made enquiries everywhere I could think of and then went to the police. It was a terrible worry as he had a War Office pass, and there was a danger it might have got into the wrong hands. He was away for a week and on the Monday morning Doris Payne, a neighbour from Fountain Road, came and said he was sitting on a

---

[17] Secretary of State for War. - Editor.

doorstep down the road. I said: "Go and tell him to come home at once."

He came and oh so dirty. I got a bath ready and all clean clothes and his best suit, gave him a good breakfast, and then had to take him up to the War Office. He had the pass, so I sent him in and I had to walk up and down until Pat came out with him. I was to take him home.

Some of the men advised Pat to let him go into the army and get some discipline, and at last he agreed to let him go. When we reached home and had our dinner, Jim went on the sofa, and fell asleep. I was going to wash all his clothes but found they were alive. I washed and boiled his shirt but had to burn most of the clothes. He had been in the east end of London, we could not get the truth of his wanderings.

In a few days he went into the Royal Munster Fusiliers and was sent to Ireland.

Jim, Pat's son from his first marriage, about 1919

128

Jim had leave at Christmas and came home with a goose. He had grown and put on weight. When he was 14 he was 5 ft 2 ins but in time he reached 6 ft. He was clean and tidy and altogether more disciplined. He was in the army until after the war. He went to Egypt, then returned and lived with his aunt in Bow.

David had been in the army since 1909 and was all through the battle on the Somme, was made lieutenant and went to India for four years. Pat had served many years in the Irish Guards and had been in the Boer War. He was a sergeant, and was proud of David.

The school was some little distance away across a main road. We moved to a house in Defoe Road to be nearer and safer for the children. The house had a long garden and was on the tram route to Wandsworth and near shops. The school and St Augustine's Church, which Mother went to, were only a little way off in a side road.

Things were very difficult. Pat was offered a post as watcher in the Customs and Excise and took it, as he had been used to an open air life, and he started off visiting ships and warehouses. We had ration cards after a while but things were scarce and we had to queue up. So much time was taken up in queues for food.

One day I had queued up for potatoes. They served a few people at a time and the others fell back to wait. A woman wearing high heels stepped back on my ankle and the heel broke my skin, just where I had a bunch of veins. I waited and got some potatoes and then we walked home. Bertha was with me. I gave the children their tea and attended to my chickens, ducks and rabbits.

I had built a chicken house and then made some rabbit hutches. The eggs and a rabbit now and then helped to feed us, and the chickens and ducks when they were past laying.

I tried to grow as many vegetables as possible, but potatoes were a failure owing to the big elm trees at the bottom of the garden, as they took all the nourishment from the soil.

When the children had gone to bed I took my stocking off. My ankle had bled and the stocking had stuck to it. I bathed it and put on a dressing, but each day it got worse. In the end I went to the doctor. He said you must rest it, but as things were that was impossible. I used to kneel to wash up etc, but it was so bad I could not get more than an hour's sleep at a time.

I kept about for 12 months and went to the doctor again, there was a big hole in my ankle. He said go back home and get to bed and stay there for six weeks! I had an oil stove beside my bed and a kettle and enamel basins I used to do the fomentations. A neighbour came over and cooked the children some dinner and sometimes Pat was home if he had been on at night.

How thankful I was for no air raids for six weeks, and then an all night one. I bandaged my leg, and got down the stairs on my seat. Pat took the children down. My ankle healed and I was thankful, as my neighbour got government work.

One Saturday night I woke and thought all my rabbit hutches had fallen, but the light from the searchlights and the noise of the Zeppelins made me rush to the children. The lights shone full in their room and gave one the notion that they could see us.

The children were too big to carry but I got Bertha and grabbed Lennie and took them down under the kitchen table, that was their shelter. It always happened when Pat was away on night work except the last raid.

130

I went shopping one morning and while I was in a shop the warning sounded. I came over faint and the shopkeeper made me sit down. When I reached home Mother and the two children were out the front looking up as shrapnel was falling. Many children did not realize the danger and used to rush and pick up hot shrapnel, for souvenirs.

I had not very much money to keep house, pay rent and coals and light for the five of us. We were always careful. Pat's trousers were cut down to make knickerbockers for Lennie, and old dresses of my sisters were passed on to me. Whenever I could get a small remnant of material in a sale I made dresses for Bertha. Sometimes they were dull colours and I embroidered them to make them pretty.

Len, aged 14 or 15 at the house at Topsham Road, Upper Tooting

131

The war was followed by a flu epidemic. Many people died, several of our friends succumbed and we all suffered apart from Pat.

In 1922 we had another bad health year. For several months I was very ill with my heart and Bertha had to cook under Mother's supervision.

When I was getting better Pat took me for a ride on the tram as far as Putney. When I returned Bertha was poorly and was restless all night. Next day the doctor came and sent her into St James' Hospital, Balham, where she was operated on for appendicitis.

The following Sunday Lennie took ill and the doctor said it could not possibly be another case of appendicitis, as it was not catching. The delay of another day meant peritonitis set in and he was operated on at the same hospital. I was sent a bill of £50 to pay for their operations. I had to pay it off at 5/- a week, as I could not afford more.

While we were living at Defoe Road Mother was diagnosed as diabetic and Bertha had rheumatic fever after her school took part in a kind of swimming gala at Balham baths. Races for swimmers were interspersed with team games for non swimmers. Bertha could not swim, and the non swimmers had to wait about. It was November. Then they walked home about one and a half miles in the rain.

Mother was not taking to her restricted diet. She hated saccharine. We tried making her cakes and puddings with it but at last she told me not to bother, as they all tasted like sawdust.

We had an unexpected visit from Mother's cousin Emma, without a bird this time. She had to share Bertha's room. Each night she took off her bedspread and did exercises. Next she brought out a ball and rolled it under the bed. Then she took up the bedspread and took a leap into bed. She told Bertha you never knew whether there was a man under the bed.

Alice (left) and Nellie at their father's grave in Tooting churchyard, 1928

David was to go to India and although Pat had spent a lot buying him things, he came one evening to ask for £5[18] as he was leaving the next day. I was not well and the children had just recovered from flu. I told him we had not got the money and he stayed till quite late.

I knew then Pat had to stay on all night, after his day, and would be very tired when he came home in the morning, but David only said: "Tell Dad to meet me at the dock and bring the money."

After that we sent on his commission parchment and he did not acknowledge it or write to us all the four years he was in India.

One evening four years later I had been out and Pat was away that night, I had just gone up to bed and taken off my shoes as my feet ached. There was a knock at the door, and I went down and there was David. I had to get him a meal and turn Bertha out of bed to sleep with me, and give him her bed. A lot of his cases came and stood in the passage.

There was no room in our little house for another man, as Mother had the sitting room, our kitchen was small and our sitting room furniture was upstairs in our bedroom. When David came we had to have Bertha in our bedroom, the other two rooms were small. Everyone was crowded and upset.

As David was determined to live with us[19] and there was not enough room he wanted me to buy a house, and I had not got money enough. He said he would have to invest and that would suit him. He had received money when he threw up his

---

[18] Altogether I think David borrowed £20. - BM.
[19] Because it was cheaper. - BM.

commission as an officer.[20] So we went house hunting and it was a business, I knew nothing about this sort of thing.

When we found one we thought suitable there was some hitch about getting vacant possession. In the end we had to meet them with their solicitors and give them the money, and they were to leave next day. Later it turned out they were Germans.

We had only seen the house with them living in it. We moved in and found floor boards loose in the dining room and underneath several tin boxes we thought had been used for their valuables.

Oh the things that had been hidden. Windows behind the blinds were cracked and broke when we tried to open them, and the next morning Mother called out to say water was coming through the ceiling on to her bed. I got Lennie to go up to the loft through the cupboard on the landing and he found the tank was leaking and old bowls they had put around were overflowing.

We had to have the plumber to empty and repair the tank. Then we found the lavatory pan was cracked and plastered up with strips of sticking plaster. Then when I moved the draining board to fill the copper, the lid had been used for firewood, and the door of the copper fire was jammed and had to be taken off with an hacksaw. It was all expense.

The house was fairly modern, mock Tudor, in Topsham Road, Upper Tooting, near Tooting Bec Common. The lounge was big enough to take all David's trophies. He put the ibex heads on the walls and on the floor he spread two large skins with mounted heads and glass eyes. One was a Himalayan bear and the other a tiger. We had to be careful not to trip over the heads when we crossed the room.

---

[20] When the Second World War broke out he rejoined the army and was a major training troops in the Isle of Man. - BM.

I soon had to supply David with money, beside the repayments we had agreed upon so that three quarters of the house was his and a quarter mine, so I had to write to the headmaster at the School of Building in Brixton, where I had placed Len for three years, and explain he would have to start earning as I was in such a fix.

So Lennie left. I bought him some tools and he got a job with a builder and carpenter. He was very good and gave me his money and I passed it on to David. David was always asking for money, he had been used to plenty in India. He began as a freelance photographer for magazines after leaving the army and spent lots of money on photographic equipment, enlarger etc.

I took a baby of three months to bring up, to help a friend of my sister Ruth's. She needed care as her mother was ill. Ruth said if anyone could manage to rear her it would be me.

Little by little baby Josie improved. We all loved her. Lennie made her a cradle out of a strong box and I lined it. Pat rocked her in it. The pram that was sent was dangerous and tipped up at the least pressure on the hood. We changed it and were soon able to take her out.

After six months she was a happy, smiling child and we were all upset when her parents wanted her back.

57. OFF TO HERNE HILL

So we were jogging along, and had been in the house just over a year, when David said he wanted his money back. He had met a young widow with two little boys and wanted to get married, and had got through all the rest of the money he received when he threw up his commission, and had no regular job. I told him I would look for a cheaper house, in the £400-500 range.

I was praying for guidance and after many inspections of houses and the blocks I asked for if not the right place, we went to look at one at Herne Hill, a district I did not know, and it seemed suitable, but until I was sure I would not make a move to buy it. I did not know how the family would get to their work and school. The Lord showed me by unmistakable signs it was right, by things coming right, and so it proved to be.

The owner of the house wanted to sell the two tons of coal in the cellar, and the fowls and sheds in the small back garden. I just could not see how I could, David had most of the money from the auction of the other house, leaving me with about £100. But my sisters Aggie and Nellie lent me some money and Mr G[21] £100 for a few weeks.

I paid Mr G and Aggie back in three weeks and Nellie kindly let me pay her back monthly. Then I was able by selling some things to pay for the coal and fowls etc. How wonderful it was to know the Heavenly Father was guiding all the business, and it was a most wonderful move.

The men and van came very early, and most of the things were in the van. Bertha, Mother and I and baby Josie with the dog (Bob) and the cat (Tiger) got into the taxi and arrived at the house about

---

[21] Mrs Gittings was a friend. - BM.

10.30. We put baby in a dresser drawer to sleep and got a nice fire going before the van and furniture arrived. Everything worked out so well.

It was a large terrace house in Shakespeare Road opposite the railway sidings. They were shut off from the road by railings, trees and grass. The shunting began at night and the trucks cannoned into one another in a series of loud collisions. After a while we got used to it and slept soundly.

There was a high wall round the garden at the back and the previous owner had cemented the middle part and built chicken sheds with small runs on three sides. There was a double drawing room with folding doors, so I gave the back half over to Mother, and we settled in and found everything had been left as promised.

The house was in good repair, but the paintwork was dark. Some doors, including the front door, were varnished and grained. This was done while the varnish was still wet. The painter took a comb and made squiggles and wavy lines to represent the grain of wood.

Mr Jones, a neighbour, suggested Len apply to be a Post Office engineer, which involved training at P.O headquarters. He was enrolled, and the station being at the end of the road it was convenient for getting to London for him and for Pat.

Soon Mother had one of her notions. This time it was rats!!! There was a cellar but no sign of rats. One of the hens had been left by herself in a shed and on one side of this leant an old door. After about 10 days or so it was moved and there was a round hole in the earth full of eggs.

I gathered them up and took them in to Mother. "Now," I said, "are you satisfied there are no rats." She looked at them cautiously and said: "Well I expect you are right, but you never know what you will find in a new house."

She could not walk very far as she suffered with arthritis, but she wanted to go out. I borrowed a bath chair. This was a basket shaped carriage which had a small wheel in front and a handle attached to a long iron rod to steer it.

One day Aggie came and suggested we take Mother to Brockwell Park near by. We climbed the hill to the house on top to see the view. Mother enjoyed it, and Bertha came to help. Going back down Bertha and I fought against the bath chair being carried away. Then we discovered Aggie was pushing it.

We wanted more growing space in the garden. We got rid of the fowls and I pulled down the chicken sheds and chopped them for firewood. I broke up some of the concrete and used it to make a small wall round the flower beds I was going to have. Horse manure was readily available as little boys with buckets were always out collecting it for sale. Tradesmen had horse drawn vehicles.

Nellie (left), Mother, Pat and Alice, at Herne Hill, summer 1928 after Mother and Alice had both been in hospital

We went to the Wesleyan Hall but after the Central Hall at Tooting it seemed so lifeless, poor singing, and it unsettled Len, and we did indeed miss our old meetings and class[22] though we found a few of God's people. I did pray for guidance as Len was not going with any desire. Just then an old friend from Tooting lent me some magazines and among them was the Witness.

I told her I liked it and she gave me another and there I found the Brethren[23] who met at Gospel Halls and this magazine mentioned a list of assemblies, to be seen at Pickering and Inglis at Paternoster Row. That was where I bought tracts, so Bertha and I went up her next half day from school.

We went round on the Saturday and found the little hall in Brixton, in a cottage, and on the Sunday we went to the gospel service, and the next Sunday we persuaded Len to go. We felt indeed the Lord had led us and the Scriptures were so faithfully taught. I had to tell the Wesleyan minister I was leaving after 31 years' membership. Soon Len desired to be baptised, and then Bertha.

While living there we had the joy of going to the Crystal Palace for Bible day. Another joy was the wonderful opportunity I had of pointing Mrs Chapman, our greengrocer's wife, to the Lord and we got to know Mrs Love, who had been to some meetings for healing and was saved, also her husband. That was in 1926, and I still write to her and hear from her at Christmas.

---

[22] The society class, held on a week night for prayer and praise. - BM.
[23] Plymouth Brethren. They do not use 'Plymouth' among themselves.- BM.

59. FATHER AND MOTHER DIE

In 1928, I heard my father was ill. He had a bed sitting room with part board in a house in Lower Tooting. I had looked after him as much as possible and he asked me for Nellie's address as I was the only one who did visit him. I told her and from then on she also used to go and see him.

I had a card to go and see Dad.[24] He had bronchitis and was very ill and thought he would die. I took some custard etc and fed him and talked to him. When he had been ill a few years before I had asked Mr Payne to visit him, and he did and read the Scripture to him. I asked him if I might read to him, and read John 3 and 14.[25] I hoped some light penetrated.

The next day I went and stayed till the afternoon. He was very ill and not able to talk. Lennie went and stayed till late. Dad gave him his watch.

The following day, Thursday, 24 May, I got over early but he was gone, poor Father. I could only leave it with the Lord, and hope that he did look to Him at last.

I had to lay him out and get the doctor's certificate and see the undertaker. He was buried in Bertie's grave in Tooting churchyard. We were all there, Aggie, Nellie, Ruth, myself, Lennie, Kathleen, Victoria, Mrs Marshall.[26] Bertha took photos of the grave in the evening.

---

[24] Much of this and the following three paragraphs is taken from diary entries for certain months in 1925-26 and 1928 at the back of the notebook, written apparently contemporaneously. - Editor.
[25] John 3 and 4 in the notebook. - Editor.
[26] A family friend who worked at Shirley Schools before her marriage. - BM.

I was troubled about him and at night when I went to bed I asked the Lord for a word and when I opened my Bible and saw these words, 'Weep ye not for the dead, neither bemoan him,' Jeremiah 22 v 10, I know they were for me that day. I do not remember reading them before although I must have as I have read the Bible through so many times.

Mother was in Lambeth Hospital then. I had been taken ill with exophthalmic goitre and after attending the hospital for some time they said I must go in. That was why Mother had to go into hospital, I could not leave her and there was no one to look after her. She would not keep to her diet, and when I was not looking sneaked into the larder and helped herself to foods she was forbidden.

Although Aggie was taking early retirement from Shirley Schools after having shingles, she was very unkind to me over it. She did not want to look after Mother. The next year I had Mother home again for about nine months.

Aggie and Ruth had bought land at Hutton, Essex. They saw the advert, visited the place and liked it. The land was going cheap in quarter acre lots. Neither had any previous connection with Essex, although Nellie had worked at Brentwood.

They were having bungalows built. Aggie had bought a quarter of an acre, and Ruth and her second husband Fred had half an acre on one side of a lane and a quarter acre next to Aggie's on the other side. Some people had bought one or two acres.

On the Saturday when Bertha and Len were home and could look after Mother, Pat and I went down by coach to see the place, expecting Ruth and Fred to be there. We found Aggie's bungalow all finished, but no one there. An old lady said she was looking after Miss Green's place. I told her I was her sister and she kindly

142

made us a cup of tea. She was Mrs Dowlty and a nice Christian woman.

Mother looked just like Queen Victoria in her old age. She used to say: "I've shrumped up." Her hair was silver and had been very long. It was cut off in hospital, to her horror. It grew again, but not as luxuriantly. Then she had to go back to hospital to have the insulin treatment. She died in hospital in October 1930, aged 82.

Bertha, Bob the dog, Mother and Ruth, about 1928

143

We were happy in Herne Hill till a man called in connection with the Census. The front doors of our houses were recessed with a deep porch and I had a hanging basket in mine. After he had finished with me, I watered the plants and overheard him questioning my next door neighbour.

He asked for the names to be checked and there were four names, but only three elderly people lived there. I asked a friendly neighbour and she told me it was the son. He came out of prison after a four year sentence for rape. He raped an 8 year old girl after which we had to move.

I was afraid for Bertha. I would never go out and leave her in the house alone. By then she was a clerical officer in the Civil Service, as she had passed two exams.

Asking the Lord's guidance I looked at several houses round the district and as before asking Him to shut out any that were not in His plan.

Then one day I was led to look at one in Streatham and it was certainly the right one. We were very near the assembly and had such happy fellowship there for some years. The dear friends we came to know and still do, though most of them have gone to be with the Lord. Bertha and Len took Sunday school classes.

Pat and I went to Hutton again when Ruth's bungalow was built as well as Aggie's. We liked the place though there were no made roads and we had to go through a wood to reach them. As well as the bungalows being built, all individual looking, some people had put up wooden huts and were camping there as if on a holiday site.

Fred was pleased to see Pat and they got on well together. They were busy cultivating the soil. It was heavy clay but grew things to perfection, especially roses. Fred had fenced round the plot next to Aggie's with posts and wire and Ruth had begun to plant it but she really had enough to do with the half acre.

We enquired about buying the quarter acre from Ruth and Fred if it was the Lord's will, as Pat was retiring in March 1935. I thought he would not be happy in town as he had no hobby. The way opened and I bought the plot, saw the builder and he began the bungalow.

Nellie had retired on pension and found a nice little two bedroom flat in Tooting, not far from us, and Eva went to live with her. She was one of the girls from the home at Hanwell and was then about 30 and also in the Civil Service. She and her sister Elsie always regarded Nellie as their mother and used to call her Little Mother.

It was nice to have Nellie near. She made her little garden quite pretty. We all loved gardening, inheriting that from Father.

We used to go down to Hutton for weekends and Bertha went down with us and saw and helped the beginning of our garden. We had enough furniture taken down to furnish one room. Nellie stayed with Aggie.

61. HARD WORK AT HUTTON

In 1934 Bertha answered the Lord's call to serve Him in Africa and went out to be a missionary with Miss Goodsell at the Garenganze Evangelical Mission in the Belgian Congo, now Zaire.

She sailed in the August, and Pat and I, Nellie and Eva and many friends from Southcroft Gospel Hall, Streatham, went to South West India Dock in London to see her off.

The bungalow was finished by Christmas 1934, so we went down, Len and Pat and I. We left our fox terrier, little Spot, with Ivy, a friend, and took our black Persian cat Beauty. We missed Bertha.

Then when we had sold the house in Streatham the new owners wanted to come in two weeks before P retired, so he went to Nellie for those two weeks and Len into lodgings in Streatham, and I went down and got all straight by the time Pat came. Spot and Beauty were with us.

Oh how we worked! We had two wells, one hard water and the other soft water. The hard water well was fed by a spring and pumped water into the house and was for drinking. The soft water was collected from rain and was for washing and washing clothes. We had hired a dowser who went round with a forked twig. He had found water for Aggie and Ruth and they had a good supply, and soon we did also.

We went to sales and nurseries and bought and planted young fruit trees, roses, shrubs and perennials, and Pat used to do the digging as he knew nothing about gardening, and when we got it all going he used to do the weeding. Aggie and Ruth had joined the Women's Institute and they had flower shows and other activities in Billericay.

I went with Ruth to a sale near by and bought some fowls and a lot of timber. Pat helped me build a shed for them and a run. Then we built a coal shed, and the council sent a letter to inform me I must submit plans for the shed. I had to attend a meeting and when I asked them which shed they meant they did not know but I was given a form for me to measure the shed and the distance from the house and any other house.

They were a lot of bunglers, as in December 1938 when Bertha came home from Africa I got a good builder to build another room and he submitted plans and had to wait their time before he got permission and could start.

Then in 1942 while the war was on and the bungalow let as I was with Bertha, they sent a notice for me to pull down the addition. I sent them word that they had passed the plans, and it was a permanent building and could not be removed without pulling down part of the main structure. Months after they said it could remain and no apology.

When the addition was built they sent me a very much increased rate, and I had to attend their meeting again, and after a lot of talk they were asking each other where this place was. One said: "Oh on the outskirts." I said: "Yes, no made road! no dust collection!! no lights!! no drainage!!" So they modified their demands.

We had made a lovely garden and such lots of roses. Pat loved roses and we had them round the lawn where the lily pond was, and over a pergola and an arch. There was a rockery and we grew all our vegetables and fruit, strawberries, raspberries, black and red currants. I learnt to graft and grafted several apple trees and a Bramley seedling, it had some nice apples. We had three pear trees, three plums and two damsons.

We had no fridge. We kept a metal safe out in the cool and hung wet cloths over it when the weather was hot. Pat spent all the

147

hours he could in the garden, cutting the lawns as well as weeding. It was so quiet and peaceful. In the summer we had our meals under the rose pergola.

A hedge marked the boundary just beyond Aggie's and Ruth's, making the lane a cul de sac. Ruth had the idea to make a path through the farm on the other side of the hedge for private use, to save going all down the lane and through a wood to catch a bus, as no one would help maintain the lane. The farm people agreed.

Fred and Pat did a lot, putting barrow loads of hard core in the lane, but no one else troubled and it got muddy and potholed. Poor Pat worked with Fred to make this other path, and it really was bad for Pat. We did not know then that his heart was bad, we did not get much benefit of the new path after all.

There was one problem going through the farm. They kept goats and the goats used to butt you and upset your shopping basket. Then it was a race to see who could get to the shopping first, you to pick it up or the goats to eat it.

Bertha at 17 (left) and at 23

In 1938 Len and Nesta were married in the October in Barnehurst, near Bexleyheath, Kent, and we were all provided with gas masks and told to take them with us wherever we went, as war was thought to be imminent, so we went up to London and then down to Kent carrying our masks. Len had managed to get a flat to rent.

The following 15 August David was born and people were leaving London, children being evacuated. So when he was two weeks old Nesta arrived with him and her mother (though her mother did not stay) and their big Airedale dog. We had to chain little Spot up and put the Airedale in the shed as they did not agree.

Len came down for the weekend, and on Sunday they went to Billericay to chapel and war was declared over the radio and then the siren went. Bertha and I fetched the pram in from the garden, we did not know what to expect.

Poor little David did not thrive and cried. Bertha had been in hospital for an operation, ligation of the saphenous vein, and she took to looking after the baby as Nesta was scared of handling him and did not know what to do when he cried. Bertha used to bath him and sing to him. Nesta did not like being parted from Len and after two or three weeks he took them back.

Bertha tried to get a post as matron in a children's home. After two attempts, and being told she was too old at 29, she spoke to a friend in the Home Office. He said there were vacancies but she would have to go in on a temporary basis as she had forfeited her established position when she left for Africa. She boarded with Mrs Love in Tulse Hill and came home for weekends.

Fred had bought Ruth a knitting machine which was set up in her spare bedroom and she soon began to turn out pants and vests for Fred, and pullovers for all the family. We were all glad as it was very cold in that part of Essex in the winter.

I bottled fruit and made jam, and stored the potatoes in a clamp. We went into Billericay once a week to shop and draw our pension. Pat and I were living on 19 shillings a week, the same amount we had had years ago after we married, and it still took ingenuity to make it go as far as possible.

My sisters came home from Women's Institute meetings with patterns for making gloves. I copied one. We bought cheap wash leather to practise on, then we were able to make kid gloves and even long furry gauntlets from the skins of Ruth's chinchilla rabbits which we had learnt to cure. Aggie and Ruth won prizes and cups for their flowers and produce.

Nellie aged 60

63. PAT DIES

In March 1940 Pat was ailing. He complained of indigestion and we blamed the pig's head I roasted instead of making brawn as usual. He wanted a roast, he loved the crackling. At last I persuaded him to see the doctor, and when we next went to Billericay I left him at the surgery and collected the pension and did the shopping.

When I got back the doctor told me Pat was suffering from auricular fibrillation and he sent him to Billericay Hospital. Pat had never had any illness and did not know what it was like to be confined to bed. They gave him sedatives which made him hallucinate and when we visited he thought he was in Ireland or the Blackwall Tunnel, anywhere but the right place.

He did not improve and I had him home and he was put to bed and told to rest, but that was the one thing he could not do. He wandered about the bungalow night and day.

Once Bertha caught him going out of the front gate in his night shirt. He would want to go out in the garden and we would put a rug on the grass near the lily pond where he could see his roses. After 20 minutes he wanted to come in again. He could not eat or sleep, and lost weight rapidly.

I was ill myself and he was sent back again to hospital for some weeks. Then we had a bad night of bombing and I got him home and had a lot of trouble to get a cab as all the people were getting their loved ones home.

He lingered on till 18 August. Bertha was home and Len had come. Oh it was a day! the Germans kept coming over and

151

dropping bombs and the sirens wailing. A neighbour had offered to go to the doctor if I let him know.

On the Saturday when Bertha came down from London, she went at once to the doctor. I had sat by Pat every night all that week. Doctor came and gave him an injection. Bertha said she would sit with her father and I went on my bed and fell asleep exhausted.

Dear Bertha sang hymns to him as that quietened him and after a rest I went in and he opened his eyes and saw me, took my hand saying "Mother." After a little while Bertha loosened my hand, and she held his. That was the last word,[27] he went quietly, just after dinner. I had cooked, for both Lennie and Bertha needed food.

Mr Braybrook, the neighbour, went to Billericay to get the doctor's certificate and had to get off his bicycle and crouch in the hedge as the Germans swooped down and machine gunned the road.

Len had to go home to Nesta and Bertha stayed with me and laid Pat out and saw to the funeral arrangements. He was buried in the pretty little churchyard at Hutton. Len and Bertha and Aggie and Ruth, my sisters, were with me. Nellie could not get to us. He was buried on Wednesday and on the Thursday Bertha had to go back to work.

She did not want to leave me there, and I knew they would both be worried if we were all separated, and the bombs were being dropped near the coast, so I went up with Bertha to Mrs Love's at Tulse Hill.

---

[27] He said "Mother" to Alice before she went to bed. It was the last word she heard. I sat up with him all night, singing his favourite hymns and holding his hand. He said: "God be merciful to me, a sinner," just before dawn. Alice was ill with kidney trouble that night. - BM.

64. RESCUING BEAUTY

Mrs Love offered her sitting room and a bedroom, and arranged with a man to move enough furniture from our bungalow to fill those two rooms.

I did not know what to do with my two dear pets. I could not take Spot as no one was allowed to take animals into public vehicles,[28] so Len got something from the chemist to put him to sleep. We were heartbroken over it. He and Beauty had always been such friends, sleeping in each other's paws and sharing their food.

It was mid morning when Len got to Hutton and he was going to dig my potatoes as well. I did not know the men Mrs Love got to move my things, she had told them there would be a lot of fruit. They helped themselves and filled bushel baskets. They were greengrocers, and brothers, but they did not pay for it.

At last they were off and I had to follow by bus and Green Line coach, leaving Len to finish and bury my dear little Spot in the garden.

I did not know what to do about Beauty and asked Ruth to feed him for me, he would not go far and the (air raid) shelter was there.

But soon Aggie wrote to say he was waiting about on the porch step and looking for me and losing weight, so Bertha and I went to the Elephant and Castle station, early on the Sunday morning. Oh what a sight of poor people who had slept on the platforms all night in the Underground stations on sacks and old coats.

---

[28] It was felt they might go berserk in an air raid. - BM.

We got to Liverpool Street station and from there went to Shenfield by train. When we got out of the station we did not know how we should get to Hutton, normally by bus. We stood by the kerb and a lady in a car stopped and asked if she could help us, and gave us a lift most of the way. We had taken some dinner, raids were going on all day but they were getting through to London.

We put Beauty in my old tin hatbox and got another lift to Shenfield station. We had to wait there, because of the heavy raids. At last we arrived at Liverpool Street station and there it was crowded with people who had been bombed out, and people trying to get to some place.

There was hardly room to stand, and one poor little woman with a baby asked us if it was our place where we stood, she wanted to find a spot to sit or lie down. Her husband was in the army and she wanted to go to her parents in the North. There was a man with a parrot in its cage. It had got uncovered and was saying: "What's the matter? What's the matter?"

The streets were littered with glass and no taximan wanted to go very far in these conditions. At last one agreed to take us. We let Beauty out in our sitting room and he knew there was another cat in the house. He stood by the door making indignant noises, but he settled down very well.

65. EVACUATED TO BOURNEMOUTH

The London Blitz started and we had dreadful raids every night and had to sleep in the cellars. The house was detached, with about 15 rooms, and there was another family living there and a little Scots lady who bought a tin helmet, as she thought a bomb might bounce off it.

There were mattresses and sleeping bags all over the cellars, and there were about 20 of us, when friends and the postman's family joined us. We used to volunteer to go up and make tea when there was a lull in the bombing. We had light, and did some knitting to take our minds off it.

Bertha was finding it difficult to travel each day. There were so few buses, especially in the evening, everyone was thumbing lifts. She travelled in a hearse, a laundry van, a removal van where all the passengers had to hang on to straps from the ceiling, and a milk float.

It was nothing for passengers to be on a bus or tram and asked to get off directly the siren went. You had to shelter where you could, often in a basement or a coal cellar.

After weeks of this bombing which continued all night, the Home Office decided to move all their staff[29] away. They were not told their destination, their luggage just bore their names.

We had to wait and when I got a little letter from Bertha it was from an hotel in Bournemouth. But it seems they were not very welcome by these hotel people, they thought a large number of people from London would bring the Germans' attention to them.

---

[29] Mainly clerical staff. - BM.

They were allowed just over £1 a week for each visitor, and the beds were not aired, the sheets were damp and torn, and there was a minimum amount of food. The H.O staff went down with flu.

One of the head officials, Bertha's senior officer, found another, friendly hotel to take them, and Bertha who had kept going and cared for those who were ill at last went down with it badly, so she was put to bed in the new Hotel Glengariffe.

When she was able to get up she told the hostess about me alone in London and she said: "Why not have your mother down for a fortnight over Christmas, I will only charge her £1 10s [£1 10 shillings] a week and she can sleep with you."

So I went down and stayed the two weeks, and met Bertha's young helper Joan who we were praying for. She was such a nice little thing. She sat at our table. All her people were B.B.C musicians.

While I was there at the Christmas party one of the head officials advised me to find a place and move down there. I had to return to London and the raids. Bertha and a missionary friend tried to find apartments, but so many people had gone down and many of the Home Office people bought houses and settled.

So we went on and at Easter Bertha came up and stayed over the weekend and thought that if I went back with her I could look round.

At that time she had a bed sitting room and boarded herself. She gave me her bed and used rugs and cushions and pillows and slept on the floor. Each day I went out and was offered unsuitable places. Some had leaking roofs, one with windows smashed, walls all scribbled over and very dirty, another with a person who wanted me to take over all responsibility.

156

At the end of the week a solicitor in the Brethren meeting we found sent a note to say two ladies in Boscombe who were his clients had apartments to let. We went to see them, they were quaint!!

They had telegrams in frames all round their drawing room walls from Buckingham Palace and Parliament. They used to send telegrams to the Royal Family on every occasion and received telegrams in reply. During the war they complained to Parliament about rationing and received telegrams back. They framed the ones they liked.

Both talked at once, they placed two chairs for us in the middle of the drawing room and two opposite for themselves and carried on two different conversations at the same time. We did not know which one to listen to or to answer.

The news came on the radio and all the national anthems of the allies were played. The Misses Hicks stood up and indicated we should do the same till the music finished. They were both in outdoor clothes and we assumed they were going out but found later they always wore coats etc to be prepared.

When I said Bertha had been in Africa, the little Miss Hicks said: "Oh I expect I have helped do up parcels Mrs Player sent out there." Mrs Player sent Bertha the first £5 for her passage money and had sent her quinine etc.[30]

We were taken upstairs and shown a nice large sitting room, a bedroom and a kitchenette. There was a bathroom on the same floor. I had to say I was afraid it would not take all my furniture. They said I could put some in an upper room, there were three or four they did not use.

---

[30] The Mission was a national and an international effort. Clothes and books were among the items sent out, as well as medicines. - BM.

I felt sure this was the Lord's leading. They said we have been praying for Christians to come. They were daughters of a clergyman and the elder, Mary, was active in the parish although her parents had been dead for some time. The younger sister Annie went out once a week, to a church service. They lived on the ground floor. There was another lady living on the same floor as us, at the back, but we seldom saw her.

The government had arranged to pay for removals and I had to get an estimate. The trouble was I had most of my furniture in the bungalow at Hutton, and the rest in the two rooms in Tulse Hill. I went to see a man at Tulse Hill and explained it to him. He said give me a list of furniture in the bungalow and the address and I will come and see what you have here.

I went down to Hutton and packed all I could. I had three tons of coal and wondered if the coal merchant would take it back and allow me something for it, when Aggie and Mrs Braybrook came and asked me to let them have it at 1s a cwt (hundredweight, or 50.9 kg).

That was £1 a ton and I had paid £3 a ton but it had to go and much else. I let some neighbours have all the good garden tools for a few shillings and gave away much I could not have taken.

Then I wanted to let the bungalow as my sister Aggie said I could not leave it vacant or it would be requisitioned by the government to house people made homeless by the bombing, and she told me a young woman whose husband was called up wanted it, but could not pay much in rent, so I let it for 15s a week and I paid the rates, leaving me with under 10s.

Soon the couple wrote saying they had had to have the hard water well cleared out at a cost of £10 as the wife was sick and thought it was the water. I paid the bill but there was nothing wrong with the water, she was pregnant.

While I was with Bertha in Bournemouth, intending going back to Tulse Hill to pack up, Mrs Love wrote to say my furniture there was on the way. It was a surprise as the man when he gave the

159

estimate said I might have to wait as there were so many removals, so I had sent the address and expected to hear from him. We went to Aylesbury Road and waited for the van and arranged for a gas stove to be fitted. That came but not the furniture.

We went round to visit Mr and Mrs Pinkham, missionaries from Italy. They had had to leave with only a small case and did not know where to go and they remembered Mrs Player, who had a boarding house or two, and she always welcomed missionaries. So she had them for a little while and then the missionary flat became vacant and they went there.

The next morning we went early and as soon as we entered the road there was Mr Pinkham waving to us. Our furniture was in and the men having some breakfast in the hall which the dear Misses Hicks had given them, and some tracts to read.

The men had to stay somewhere near Southampton as there were raids at night so they came on in the early morning. They had been so careful, and brought the eggs and all the things out of the sideboard.

We had come away leaving everything expecting to go back and pack up. Mrs Love was very cross and said I had planned it and if I wanted my cat I must come and get him. They would have liked to have kept him. It meant a long and tiring journey, as I had to go from Bournemouth to Waterloo and then get another train to Tulse Hill, and walk.

I took my hatbox again and brought him to Bournemouth. He was heavy but Mr Pinkham kindly met me at Bournemouth station and helped carry him, and we got a bus to Boscombe and home.

Buses and all other public transport were curtailed during the war for various reasons, shortage of staff and petrol, and people had to work longer. Many of the drivers were elderly or women.

Bertha used to have to walk home from work very often, it was two miles from Bournemouth to Boscombe. She liked to see the sea, although the beaches were all fenced off with barbed wire in case of invasion, and it was the only chance of getting fresh air.

Handwritten notices were everywhere in the house. There was a notice on the porch door to shut it before opening the house door, and another on that door reversing the process. In the bathroom another notice said no more than five inches of water were allowed.

This place was off bounds unless the sisters supervised. The old vicar, their father, had a fatal stroke in there. Once a week, on Friday, they would come up and camp outside while I had a bath. Bertha did not use it. During the week the Home Office staff could use one of the bathrooms at the hotel where they had the office.

The toilet was the old fashioned kind with a large mahogany box seat and a white china pan with Windsor Castle depicted in blue in it, and a hand pull from a hole beside the pan. This had a notice telling the occupant not to pull it up too far. There were three toilet roll fixtures each with a name, Hicks, Mayhew (the other tenant), and Mullen.

Under the stairs they had a Morrison air raid shelter. We only used it once. Miss Mary told me to come downstairs as there was a heavy raid going on. We were asked to squeeze in with the two sisters. Bertha said something hard was sticking in her back, and

Miss Mary said it was an oak box containing all her dear father's sermons.

We were quite near our meeting in Drummond Road and found very happy fellowship there. They were having meetings in the week for men of the forces who were billeted in hotels before being sent to fight abroad, and a canteen was open for them.

On Tuesday there were generally about 70 men, and they had a supper of tea and sandwiches and cake, and they could write letters, play draughts or chess, or read, and at the close there was an epilogue.

We all found some service in that time of need. Bertha helped and did the washing up etc. Soon we met the other people from various Ministries who were evacuated. Many Drummond Road members took them home at weekends because the young staff were often homesick.

We had some of the girls from the Home Office to tea on Sundays and took them along to the meetings. Bertha's helper Joan always came and we knew the Holy Spirit was working in her heart. She belonged to a church and had been confirmed and thought that made her a Christian so was quite annoyed at first to hear people called sinners, she did not think she was a sinner.

But the light shone in and one evening one of the Brethren spoke to her and she said she had come to the Lord. She was so happy, then she used to come along to help in the canteen.

One Saturday evening she went to a dance with some of the office girls and danced with a young man. Presently she was inviting him to the hall. He said: "Oh if you go there I'm surprised at you coming to this sort of thing." Poor Joan! She said: "I've only just begun to be a Christian and did not know," because at her church they had dances and whist drives. She asked him to go to the hall and he came but the world was his attraction.

Joan grew in grace and with two other converts was baptised at Drummond Hall after telling her people. She used to teach in the Sunday school. Bertha used to speak to the women's Bible class at the YWCA [Young Women's Christian Association] and I used to read to a blind lady[31] in the nursing home near by.

We used our powdered egg and dried milk to make cakes, they were not too bad, and there was an eggless cake that was very palatable if you could get some dried fruit to go in it. A friend taught me to use fresh fruit instead, apples, gooseberries, plums and blackberries.

There was a great fuss about rose hip syrup being a good source of vitamin C. It was much advertised as being something people could make for themselves, although it could also be bought in chemists' and grocers' shops. We went beyond Christchurch, five or six miles away, and gathered lots of wild rose hips and made syrup.

Bertha was told of a piece of garden she could use at Christchurch. We took some tools and went by trolleybus and found the place, but it was terribly hard work. Later we were told that a postman and a butcher had tried to dig it and had given up. We sowed vegetable seeds but got very little produce.

---

[31] There were two blind ladies. - BM.

163

68. SHE WILL NOT WORK OR WALK AGAIN

Then Bertha was very ill with thrombosis. The doctor when she went to see him just bandaged her leg and told her to carry on as it was war time and it was not patriotic to be ill.

By the next night she was in agony and then he sent her into the government nursing home on the West Cliff, west of Bournemouth Pier.

I went down to see her, she had sand bags down each side of her from her armpits to her feet and cradles over her body, so she could not move.

After about two weeks she thought I might go up and stay with Len and Nesta as she would be there for some time, and there were so many of her office friends going in to see her I did not see much of her when I went.

So I went up to Barnehurst, and when I came back she was worse than when I left. I had to go and see the doctor who told her to carry on and he said: "Oh I'm afraid your daughter will not work again. She will not walk again."

This was on the Saturday. On Sunday morning after the meeting Mr Laws, an elder, said if she should need to see a specialist to let him know. On Monday when I saw the doctor he said yes but Bertha said she could not afford one. I went to a friend to ask her for Mr Laws' address.

It was a long way out and I went as far as I could by bus and then began to walk. I saw a greengrocer delivering goods and asked him where it was. He said a good way but if you wait about I will drive you in.

I was so worried and had to wait until Mr L came home. I had lunch with him and his wife and they were so kind. They said they would pay for a specialist. Mr Laws took me back home in his car, he was allowed petrol as he used to take elderly people to the services. They got a specialist at once to see Bertha and he understood her case and altered her treatment.

Len aged 28

69. TO BARNEHURST

Just after this Bertha told me all the Home Office staff were to go back to London. I wrote to Len, I did not know where to go or where to look for apartments. Len heard of part of a house near him and asked me to send £1 1s to secure it as a first week's rent.

There was the business of getting estimates. I did not know quite what I had to do and had to ask Bertha, and I'm afraid it was a worry but I had no direct contact with the Home Office.

In a short time I had packed up and as my cat Beauty had had so many long train journeys and he was not used to children and was getting old, I did not take him. Miss Hicks was very fond of him and I knew he would have a good home and be loved, so I left him with them.

Bertha was improving but it was a long illness, over four months. Dear Miss Pickering and Miss Foulds, two members of the meeting, were having Bertha for convalescence.

My furniture was packed in the van and that night I slept in one of Miss Hicks' beds and after breakfast Miss Mary saw me off to London. I had dinner with Len and Nesta and the furniture came and I got all fixed. Things that would not go into the house went into the shed. I had the front bedroom, and the downstairs rooms.

I was there some weeks before Bertha was brought home and what a change. She was still very weak. She had lost four stone in weight and could wear my clothes. People did not recognise her.

There was a nice garden, and I bought some wood and made

166

rabbit hutches and kept rabbits. But when it came to eating them we were unhappy, so sold them.

Little David used to come along to see us, Nesta was expecting another baby. Our meeting was a long way off at Welling. We used to walk to Bexleyheath and then get a bus to Welling. I got to know Mrs Stephens, one of the members, and after we came to Bath had her to stay a fortnight, after her husband died.

The station was practically at the end of the road, and Bertha used to travel to the H.O by late train and return early so as to get a seat, having to rest. The task she had left had been done by several other people and left in a mess and they wanted her to pick up the pieces. After a while she went to her principal Mr Kelsey and asked to be released to do war work, as she was doing routine work. He had been with her at Bournemouth and thought she ought to work with people. He rang the Probation Department and sent her for an interview.

She was accepted for training after going before the selection board. That took nine months, at Liverpool, Nottingham and Sheffield, and finishing up in London at Lambeth for a further three months.

During this time Nesta went into the nursing home and had her baby, Diana, in 1943, and each day I went along and ran the home for Len and little David. It was a long day as Len went to visit Nesta in the evening and it meant staying, then I had my home, rabbits to feed and clean out and my cat Toodles to look after. We got Toodles as a kitten one afternoon from an advert we saw in a shop. We missed Beauty and when we went to the address in the advert there were several kittens and this little black kitten climbed all over me and clung on so I said: "This is the one!" We had to travel by two buses and he did not like it and cried so much that we walked with him the last part of the journey.

167

70. TOODLES

Toodles was such a clean kitten and so lively. He would put himself to sleep in the Morrison shelter. This he did the first evening. We missed him and looked all over and then found him curled up in the middle of the bed in the shelter.

When he was bigger and I was alone in the raids he used to spring up and jump at the beams of the searchlights and try to catch them.

I used to make soft toys for children as a hobby and he did not like these, and would get them if he could and throw them down. Once I had made a nice lot of golliwogs and rabbits etc and put them in the sitting room. I must have left the door open, and when little David came he went in and exclaimed: "Oh Nana!! see what Toodles has done!" The toys were all thrown on the floor.

He always got my slippers and would bring them downstairs, bumping them on each stair as he came. Even when I put them on top of the wardrobe he got them.

One day we went to Gravesend and when we came back could not at first make out what had happened to him. He had got the sticky fly paper down from the gas bracket where it hung and it was all stuck to his fur and he had tried to pull it off.

Oh he was a sight. We had to use what grease we had, not much in a war like ours, and then when we got the sticky paper off, wash him.

One morning I had put my vest to air on the fireguard and went into the other room to hear the news on the radio. Suddenly he was dashing up the hall and I smelt burning fur. He had jumped at

168

the flames and knocked the guard into the fire so my vest was burnt and so was he, a big patch on his flank.

I used to go to the meeting and one Sunday morning when I came home he was missing. I went along the road and asked some children if they had seen him, later they brought him and I gave them some pennies. This happened several times so I had to stop paying for his return. He found his way out over the bay window, jumping from my bedroom.

He was a wonderful cat. I brought him to Bath.

Pat and Alice, after Pat had retired, pictured about 1937

In 1944 Bertha was appointed a probation officer at Bath and went there in June. She came to fetch me because of the 'doodle bugs' or flying bombs.

They were frequent and without warning and my front door had the locks blown off and my bedroom ceiling came down and windows cracked. We were told to report the damage and I went along to the place and just as I was almost there the siren went and everyone hurried as there was a shelter near by.

I just walked quietly as I knew if I hurried I might have an heart attack, as I had one a few nights previously. So I prayed and walked. Some people said you were slow coming. They had heard of but not seen anyone take it quietly.

The next day Bertha came from Bath to fetch me and we had to cross London in an air raid to get to Paddington station. I carried Toodles in my old hatbox, and oh the crowds fleeing from London. When the train came in everyone was pushing and trying to get in. We were crowded in and most of us falling asleep, we had been kept awake so much.

When we arrived at Bath Bertha got a taxi and we went to Bloomfield Avenue where she had a bed sitting room. She told me it would be quite quiet and to go to bed and I slept all the afternoon. When I woke at a knock on the door Mrs Heath, the landlady, came in with some clean towels and said: "Where's the cat?" I looked round, he was on a shelf that made an hanging wardrobe.

One of the magistrates kindly sent a camp bed and blankets. I had left in such a hurry and left the house and everything just as it was.

We were in the bed sitting room for four months and the evenings began to get cold. Once we went to Clevedon for a little bus ride and picked up some pieces of wood on the beach. We brought them home and burnt them to warm us. All the time there I cooked on a gas ring and even made some jam.

Bertha had been promised a flat or house with her appointment and after a lot of difficulties we got a council flat in a large house in Wells Road. Just then the landlady at Barnehurst wanted her house and for me to remove my furniture and Mrs Heath told us they were moving and we would have to go.

Every Sunday we used to walk down to Manvers Hall (chapel) and when we came back Toodles waited at the end of the road near Bear Flat. Then one day he was missing. We thought he might have followed us to Wells Road as we had been to look at the flat. We advertised and went everywhere calling. Someone must have taken him and tried to keep him but after about 10 days he came home and how pleased he was to find us.

Everyone was fond of Toodles. When we were settled in the flat Mr and Mrs Adams, who were also tenants, became very fond of him and would open their dining room window to let him in. He used to walk on the hot water pipes along the hall. When we first went into the flat there were a lot of mice and Toodles was kept busy. He cleared our flat and was even asked to go in next door as their cat did not catch them.

One night Mrs Adams' son wanted to show us some films he had taken and Toodles would jump at the moving figures on the screen, so they shut him out. Later when Mrs Adams went into her bedroom we heard her say: "We have been burgled." Cupboards and drawers were open, and the contents of drawers spread about. Mr Adams' ties were all on the carpet, handkerchiefs and scent bottles and trinkets were everywhere.

It was Toodles. He had fished things out with his paw. He could always empty a drawer if he could get his paw in. When he was shut in or stopped from doing something he wanted he would open the table drawer in the kitchen and remove all the smaller cooking implements and lay them on the table, one at a time.

When we lived at Hawthorn Grove, Combe Down, he picked up mange from a stray cat and we had to have him put to sleep.

Ruth (right) with her daughter Kathleen, 1930s

In 1949 I had shingles in my head and face and was very ill for months. I passed my 70th birthday in bed and much pain. The doctor only gave me morphia for the pain and it went on and on.

Bertha got a little retired nurse from Norton St Philip to come and stay a month, then Bertha and Mrs Franklin, our help who came twice a week, moved my bed into the dining room to be warmer and nearer the kitchen, it was so far to my room and it was a north room. Then she got Mrs Matthews, a friend from the meeting who used to do some nursing, to come and look after me during the day.

She heard of Dr Reeves from several people and went to him and told him about me. He kindly came the next morning and thoroughly examined me and sent blood for testing, tried vitamin B and found out I did not absorb it from food and began giving me injections, daily at first and then three times a week. He sent for a specialist who ordered violet rays and did not think I would get over it but die in a few weeks.

Dr Reeves was wonderful and became my G.P. He told me I would always need vitamin B injections.[32] It was good Bertha could do this when I was a little better.

We had a neighbour, a rather eccentric Irish lady, who called and said to Bertha that if she needed help laying me out she should hang a white towel out of the dining room window. She was good hearted though and brought me a bottle of whisky at Christmas and when I was better in the March gave us Christmas dinner, because we had missed it.

---

[32] She had the injections for the rest of her life. - BM.

Although I recovered I had scarring to my eyes and forehead, and always pains in my head and eyes, and I could not bear a draught or cold wind.

I could not see to read or do much. Bertha bought a second hand piano and I could play hymns by ear. This was a great joy. Len gave me a harmonica. Then I thought I could crochet wool knee rugs and this was another occupation.

Bertha belonged to the Soroptimists and in the summer made enquiries among her friends and heard of a cottage she could rent for two weeks at Wrington. Miss Jewell, a friend, drove us there in her car. We had a nice holiday and the neighbours were kind.

The following Christmas we invited Mr Raymond and Dorothy, Miss Downton, Alastair and Bunty and Audrey Burrows to tea. We had a nice party and we ended by all singing hymns and carols. Mr Raymond was a good singer and always started our hymns at morning meeting. He was ill soon after and died of bronchitis.

174

We were moving as I could not wear my glasses and there were so many stairs, about 30 down to the coal cellar or garden, and I could not go out alone. I had to go into hospital for a day or two for a check up and while in there Bertha heard of some people at Twerton who would exchange their council house with us.

We had to sell a lot of furniture. Bertha had a very nice bedroom suite but it was big and that had to go with the mahogany dining table I had had so many years. Chairs and bed settee, hall stand, gas fires, rolls of lino and lots of other things I had to part with.

Miss Jewell took me to Mrs Date's for the day and Bertha and Dorothy, a friend from the meeting, got the house straight before I went there about tea time. It was a nice house and garden with a field at the end of the garden. Dorothy wanted to live with us, her parents had died and all the rest of the family were married, and she had to sell the house and furniture except what she wanted to keep.

Alastair helped her to bring some things and the removal men brought her chest of drawers, bedstead, settee and chairs, and grandfather clock. Her boxes of china etc had to go into the shed. She stayed with us for a time and then went to a cook's post at Southstoke, an annex of the orthopaedic hospital for children. She could have her furniture there.

We enjoyed the terraced garden and while there had Grace from Streatham to stay with us for a fortnight's holiday with her mother Mrs Davis. We had a little dog once more, a little smooth fox terrier named Natty. She had one puppy we called Caruso. Natty used to sing and we thought her son should have a singer's name. When he grew up we could not keep the two so we let Miss Allen, a friend, have Natty.

Alice at Hutton with Spot

74. COMBE DOWN

We had some bad neighbours the latter part of the time making us uncomfortable and when things got worse we asked for a transfer. They agreed if we would take a smaller house, so once again I had to part with furniture. Miss Allen was wanting to furnish another room and bought it all, dining chairs, screen, arm and rocking chair, etc.

We were given a house in Hawthorn Grove, Combe Down, then a village south west of Bath.[33] It was just built and there was no fencing or hedge round the garden. It was a corner site of about a quarter acre and just a rough field. Bertha heard of a man who would dig it up and he charged £9 and left it in great clods and very rough. It took a long time to break it down.

I planned the garden and we made a rockery and divided the back with an hedge across halfway for a lawn and a vegetable garden at the bottom, behind the hedge. We had raspberries and black currants. Bertha bought a morello cherry tree and some plums, and had some posts put in for a pergola and planted some nice climbing roses, also a passion flower round the porch in front.

We worked very hard and grew all our vegetables and many people stopped to admire the garden. Dorothy helped me with the weeding and I took a prize for the second best garden on the estate. It was presented at the Pump Room and Dorothy went with me to receive it.

Bertha and her friend Nellie Coles went to Keswick for the Convention held in July for the furtherance of spiritual life and they went up to London and spent the night at one of the YWCA

---

[33] Now part of the city. - BM.

homes and got the train to Keswick. They had a wonderful time but on the journey home their train broke down. Bertha had a sprained ankle and Mr Gay, a friend and the assistant clerk to the court, was to meet them at Bath station but heard there would be some hours' delay.

I watched from her bedroom window until all the lights went out except the ones on the main road, and watched for car lights along the Bradford Road. At last one came and turned in to Fox Hill after midnight.

Alastair Davidson had been to the Convention from Fegans Homes,[34] Bucks, and had taken a missionary who was on leave and back at Fegans. They became engaged and were married at the chapel at Fegans. Bertha, Dorothy and I went to their wedding by taxi. I felt so ill and could not eat anything. Later Alastair and Gill went out to Kalimpong, North India, and were out there some years looking after a children's home.

Dorothy left Southstoke and went up to her sister in law Edith's in London, she got a post at the Royal Free Hospital as diet cook.

As time went on I found the garden too much. After planting out cabbages one evening I had a lot of pain and it continued but I tried not to let Bertha know as she and her friend Nellie were planning to go to Lynmouth, Devon, at the end of the week, but I could not go on and when she came home to tea had to tell her.

She rang the doctor and he sent for the ambulance and I was sent to hospital. Their holiday was cancelled and they visited me every day. This was in September 1957.

When I came out and doctor came to see me he said you must give up this gardening, no wonder you were ill.

---

[34] Christian homes for orphans and needy children. - BM.

178

75. THE FIRS

After much thought and prayer we were led to look at 19 The Firs. Bertha had seen quite a few places, but I had asked the Lord if possible we might find something in Combe Down to be near the chapel and the many dear friends we knew. It is so much harder when you are older to settle in a fresh place and make new friends.

It was a wonderful answer to prayer when I saw the house and the conservatory though the garden was very small. I knew each year I would be less able to cope with it.

Bertha had been wanting to buy a house for some time, and it was a large Edwardian terrace house facing a field. Mr Tucker[35] kindly advised Bertha to buy it and helped us in every way.

On the moving day Bertha's friend Nellie came to help us and Bertha took me and Caruso to dear Mrs Tucker's to spend the day with them and called for me after tea. The dining room looked so cosy with a bright fire and all the furniture in place. Then I went up to my bedroom and that was all ready, and a nice little fire. This was December 1957.

It was so private after the house in Hawthorn Grove and very convenient to the field so that we could take Caruso for a little run. It needed modernising and renovating and Bertha was soon papering and painting. A plumber and a carpenter worked on it and we were very comfortable and happy there.

We had nice neighbours. Mrs Elliott next door was aged and I went in to see her and have a little talk. She was pleased to see

---

[35] A builder and unpaid minister of a little Baptist chapel known as Union Chapel. There were other preachers there as well. - BM.

me. It was so good to be near Union Chapel and I enjoyed Mr Tucker's ministry. We went down to Manvers Hall on Sunday morning and Bertha went down again in the afternoon to take her Bible class, so we liked to go to chapel in the evening.

Bertha had bought me two wooden slat forms from the army surplus store, Bests, to put in the conservatory for shelves for my plants. They did very well, one above the other, it was so nice to be able to keep all the geraniums and pot plants through the winter. I could sit in the conservatory even when it was raining and I used to take my books and crochet and sit surrounded by flowers.

I could crochet without having to look and made wool knee rugs for missionaries and continued to do so even when I became more confined to bed, from 1963. I also painted, I had a wooden reading support on legs which could be put over my knees in bed and used as an easel. I sent the rugs all over the world, with my paintings. I made my own cards and notelets to use for correspondence.

We had Grace Heywood, a former missionary, to stay with us and enjoyed her company and news of Africa. Bertha's friend Nellie used to come and spent the night with us on Thursdays and also weekends and she played Scrabble with me. It was near Rainbow Wood and easy to get out in the country round about. A favourite ride was to Wellow and on the way we would stop and picnic. We found the wild asparagus the Gypsies used to sell.

David was in the RAF doing his National Service and Nesta rang to ask if we could put him up one night on his way back from leave. [Len and Nesta and family had moved to Weymouth from Barnehurst.] We put him in the sitting room. Nellie was with us. He came quite late by taxi and went off after breakfast. He was so tall and made me feel small.

He chose the RAF hoping he would learn to fly but they made him secretary to the Commandant and he was sent to Gan on the Addu Atoll, the most southern of a chain of islands running southwest of Sri Lanka 40 miles below the Equator, an RAF post which no longer exists.

He was happier doing outdoor work and when he came home he went into Dorset council's quantity surveyor's office. Diana went into the Civil Service in Dorchester when she left school and was a clerk in Agriculture and Fisheries.

Len and Nesta on their wedding day at Barnehurst in 1938

Bertha and her friend Nellie had been to Guernsey for two weeks and had a lovely time. They took some snaps, all very lovely. We three had stayed at Sidmouth at the Christian Alliance for Women and Girls and one year we went to Minehead and left Caruso in the kennels, but when we went to Paignton we took him and had a furnished cottage.

Then Nellie suggested that the next holiday, in 1959, I should go with them to Guernsey and they also wrote to Dorothy and we all went, Dorothy by air and we three by boat from Weymouth. Nesta and Diana came down to see us off and gave me a box of sweets.

We had a lovely time and they hired a bath chair to take me to the bus and left the chair at a garage near the bus stop so I was able to go to all the outings. The island is beautiful. We stayed at Miss Collings' guest house. The lanes were full of wild flowers and there were rock roses, lupins and mesembryanthemums cascading down to the sea.

Once they took me over to Herm by boat and there were so many tiny yellow roses growing on the ground you could not avoid stepping on them, and bluebells like a sheet of misty purple clothing the cliffs by a beach covered with shells.

In May 1961 we had arranged to take Caruso to the kennels as we were going to Guernsey again and were having a caravan on a farm. But Caruso had got so hysterical while Bertha was ill for a month with a cholecystectomy.

We had a woman who had done some housework for us many years before. She used to take Caruso out twice a day and we did

182

not know till some time afterwards she used to drag him along and would not let him stop for the calls of nature. So he became hysterical and short tempered.

We tried taking him out by car as we used to, but he was so trying that Bertha enquired at the RSPCA [Royal Society for the Prevention of Cruelty to Animals] about what to do as we felt he would not be accepted at the kennels. We were advised to take him down. It was a dreadful journey with him barking all the time and we were advised to have him put to sleep.[36]

It was so upsetting and Bertha promised to buy me a Siamese kitten. She did but had to leave it till we came home from Guernsey.

He was such a clever dog. He would sing all through the happy birthday jingle. He would shut the door after him.

One day I was just finishing lunch and he got out of his basket in the breakfast room and fetched the hassock I used when I had an afternoon nap. He then fetched the lap robe (knee rug) and found my hot water bottle and laid that down. Next he came back dragging the telephone directory.

He knew that I sat by the fire with my rug, hot water bottle and a book each day after lunch.

---

[36] The RSPCA thought he ought to go to a farm and live rough but he had always been a pet and we could not agree to this. The vet suggested he be put to sleep, not the kennels, which were in the country and run by a kindly old gentleman. - BM.

When we came back from Guernsey we brought back a little Siamese cross kitten. He was black with blue eyes and Bertha called him Cobo after Cobo Bay. He was so good all the long journey by sea and train and car. I had him on my lap all the way in a tomato chip basket. Dear Mr Tucker met us with his car at Bath station and when we got indoors he opened the basket and out jumped little Cobo.

On the Saturday we went for the little kit Bertha had promised me. It was a poor little specimen and was so scared of Cobo. All day he clung to me and would not be friends with Cobo who was a lively little kitty. On the Monday Cobo chased Chula about and boxed him up and down stairs and that made them friends.

Miss Allen had Natty, Caruso's mother, eight years and when she died they missed her so much they rang us to ask if they could borrow Caruso but it was just after we had to part with him.

Mrs Elliott next door died and her house was sold and made into flats. Now we had flats each side of us.

Our David was to be married to Pat Samways in March 1964 and we asked Mr Pow who had retired to take us there and back as he had done to Alastair's wedding. It all went off well and there were a great number of guests at the Pier Restaurant for the reception. We met many friends and some of Nesta's family. Bertha took some nice snaps outside the hall.

In March 1966 Diana married Alan Tune. We made arrangements for Mr Pow to take us again as I'm 86. The weather was good and we were there quite early and saw Diana dress. She looked very lovely coming in with her father and the service was very nice.

Diana had to follow Alan back to Singapore as he had short leave from the RAF for their wedding. He looked very cold while the snaps were being taken outside the hall, he must have felt the cold after Singapore.

In December 1966 Bertha had to go into the Mineral Water Hospital[37] for treatment for arthritis. She had been having various treatments at St Martin's, the large general hospital near us at Combe Down, but was no better. She went in for a month and was on a strict diet with treatment and bath. She was better and lost a lot of weight. She could come home in the day if not having treatment or expecting the doctor.

When Diana and Alan came home they bought an house in Lincolnshire where Alan's station in the RAF was, and in December 1967 Hazel May was born, my first great-grandchild.

On Easter Monday 1968 we went down with Bertha's friend Nellie to spend the day at Weymouth with the family. Diana and Alan and baby had come all the way from Stamford and we had a real family party for tea. I had all my family of nine round the table and Len took a snap of four generations. She was a lovely baby.

We have had a nice summer so far in 1968 and Bertha has taken me out quite a lot, she had a week off. We went to Longleat and saw the lions. They were so natural in the open walking about and playing and one was lovely like my orange Persian cat Candy,[38] he sat up by a tree.

We went to Wincanton and I bought a new carpet for my room and my dear Bertha bought me some rugs, very pretty.

---

[37] The Royal National Hospital for Rheumatic Diseases, built over a hot spring in the centre of Bath, known widely by its old name. - BM.

[38] One of my probationers brought a kitten to me. Alice adopted him and got very fond of him. He got on well with the other two cats. - BM.

In July 1968 I suddenly felt very shivery and as if cold water was running down my back. I managed to fill an hot water bottle and undress and get into bed. When Bertha came home she said: "What's the matter?" I said I don't feel well, so she took my temperature and phoned Dr Jameson.

He came and sounded me and said pneumonia.[39] He left antibiotics to be taken every four hours and Bertha sat up with me most of the night.

I went on with the antibiotics and got well enough to get up in the afternoons. Len and Nesta came. Bertha had bought me a blue dress, very easy to slip on without fastening, just a little zip at the back.

One afternoon I had the same symptoms and got back to bed. When doctor came he said it was the same again and I went over the same ground but when I thought I was on the mend I had a lot of pain lower down and Dr King came to see me and examined me and said gall bladder.

And again the third time the same symptoms and then Dr Jameson came in the morning and said you will have to go into hospital. The ambulance came and I was taken to ward 16, St Martin's, and was there a month. They x rayed me and put me on a fat free diet. Poor Bertha looked so tired and worn out when she visited me and I felt it would be better for her if I were home and kept to the diet.

---

[39] She had gall bladder trouble and a touch of bronchitis. But from 1960 she had pneumonia twice and went to hospital on several occasions with kidney trouble, diverticulitis and valvular heart disease as well as gall bladder trouble. - BM.

The ambulance brought me home in November. It had been so warm in the hospital that I got a chill, and had to stay in bed. Bertha was very overstrained and Dr King said she must get away for a change,[40] and spoke of getting me into a convalescent home. But with our three lovely pussies, we couldn't leave them like that.

We thought of Dorothy and Bertha wrote to ask if she was free would she come and stay with me. She came and they went to Bournemouth for a week. It was a trying time but we came through. I had my 89th birthday and Dot went back to Torquay for Christmas. She had gone there to be housekeeper to an elderly widower and a few months later married him.

I was getting up a little each day but it got increasingly difficult as I was so distended I could not wear any corsets and as it got worse and worse if I sat up for more than an hour I asked Dr Jameson if I could have some sort of support.

He said no it would not help me, but when Dr King came and examined me, he said yes you must see Dr Dixon, the doctor I had been under at St Martin's. So I was taken by ambulance to the hospital and was examined by Dr Dixon and x rayed several times.

Then the belt was ordered and the lady fitter came and took my measurements and in July I had the belt. It made a great difference and I have been able to get up and stay up for about four hours.

Bertha was struggling on with her work but getting worse with pain and disability and Dr Dixon said she must go into hospital again. She had been in for a month in 1966 with arthritis and again after Christmas 1967 and now in 1969, when she was also suffering

---

[40] I had been very ill with osteoarthritis. - BM.

187

from spondylolisthesis. Dear Mrs Tucker offered to come and stay with me.

Dear Mr Tucker had been taken ill suddenly in the March with a deadly virus and was taken to the hospital but fell asleep in the Lord. It was such a shock to us all, he was greatly beloved, a true servant of the Lord. How we all missed him and dear Mrs Tucker more than anyone can tell, as they were so much together.

Alice's grandchildren David and Diana about 1945

188

Dr Dixon had a long talk with Bertha and said she was not fit for work. She came home after a month's treatment and her principal rang up to say she was not to go back, she was invalided out of the service. She would be put on half pay and sick pay until she got her pension in the October and the old age pension in December 1970.

She had to go to the office and deal with enquiries and paperwork until they appointed a replacement. She was presented with an electric sewing machine from the probation officers and a gold watch from the magistrates.

She was told she should not do the stairs, so began looking for a bungalow but found nothing suitable in Bath. She and her friend Nellie thought they could manage a few days' holiday and hoped to go to Sidmouth but although it was October they could not get fixed up.

Then Bertha said to Nellie: "Shall we go out like Abraham not knowing where we are going?" and they did and wonderfully found a place some miles from Chard where they took them and garaged the car. They were looking about for a cottage or bungalow and spent the Sunday with Alastair and Gill in Chard.

We were getting adverts of houses etc from several places. One morning just before Christmas one came and I read it over and said to Bertha this looks like our place, and she read it and agreed. She said shall I write and ask Gill to look at it for us as it's so near Christmas. She wrote the letter and posted it.

In a few hours one came from Gill, the letters had crossed but Gill had already been over the bungalow and claimed it in the Lord's name for us. Then she phoned and said Bertha must come down and see it and make an offer that week. Bertha asked Nellie if she could go with her as they were buying it between them.

They saw it and it was just right. It was a three bedroom chalet bungalow with an upstairs bedroom, it had been built six years, and had a large garden. In front there was a fine view and at the back fields.

They paid a deposit and fixed up with a solicitor and started all the business, it was Christmas week. Then came the P.O strike and no letters could get through.

One of the cards Alice used to make. This one was drawn with crayons and coloured pens

80. SO MANY PRAYERS ANSWERED

Bertha advertised our house for sale in the Bath Chronicle. It came out about 4 pm and on the first day there was a lady on the doorstep half an hour later. We had gone to bed when a man called at 10 pm and asked to see over the house. He came again at 9 next morning and he was the buyer.

Before anything was finalised two ladies called to see the house. They were spiritualists. They wanted to know if birds came down the chimneys and whether the house shook. One went into the breakfast room and into the kitchen, looking at the ceiling for several minutes. Her friend said: "Don't go into a trance now, Blanche. We haven't time."

They went upstairs and began to suggest where they would place their furniture. Suddenly one enquired if I read books from the mobile library. She thought it was an unlucky sign. They also enquired where we went to church. Blanche thought she saw a raven in the attic. Her friend kept touching the walls and doors, as she said there were vibes to warn them. They did not want to buy!

We could not get any news from Chard, we just got ready in faith and Bertha sold a lot of things including my bookcase and her old sewing machine.

She wrote to Pat and David. We had the phone taken away as doctor said the car was more necessary for Bertha and there was a garage so that was little extra expense. Len and Nesta were surprised when they came and found we were moving and thought we could have phoned, but she had enough trouble getting in touch with the solicitors.

At last in March everything was settled. I had to go into hospital for two days and nights while the moving went on.

Bertha and Nellie had an hectic time with the three cats crying in the car tied up in sacks. The vet said they would be alright after the tablets, but the moving men were late and then when they got to Chard they could not get the key and had to wait so long they had only just got it when the furniture came. The neighbours gave them some tea, but they did have a day.

Bertha came back for me on the Saturday afternoon and poor Nellie looked so sad as she had to go home to Bath and know we were farther away. David and Pat came and spent the day with us. David moved the two plum trees and planted them down the side, he put the stair carpet down and fixed all the fixtures and did a lot of little jobs for us.

Now we are here it's a lovely place and Len and Nesta have been to see us. I have a bedroom looking out on to the back garden. There are three apple trees. The neighbours are friendly and ask if they can do any shopping for us, the chapel is about half a mile away.

Waking up in the morning we hear the birds singing, rabbits run about and a squirrel visits. In the meadow opposite is a cock pheasant and five hen pheasants and a beautiful wild duck has taken refuge on the front lawn. There is a farm up the road a little way and morning and evening the cows come along the road to pasture.

Nellie brought her niece and her sister May to see us in the summer, but poor May looked very ill. Nellie also managed a day by train and then May got weaker and from Nellie's letters we knew she could not go on and then just Christmas week Miss Amber, our neighbour, came in the evening to tell Bertha she was wanted on the phone.

192

May had died in Nellie's arms as she was trying to lift her 23 December 1971. Nellie's other older sister was also an invalid and she had died before May.

Bertha went up and fetched Nellie after the funeral. Nellie looked worn out, she thought she would go back in three weeks, but we persuaded her to stop three months and get rested before she had all the business of settling all her affairs. It was a lot to see to and we prayed all would go well, especially the selling the house.

She did not want to advertise, so I asked the Lord to send someone to buy it and He did, a young Christian man who was getting married. It took time and was unusual as the building societies don't like lending money for old houses but the council did and it all went through.

What furniture she wanted she sent down, then in the evening the young man who was buying the house brought her down by car.

July 1972: I'm in my 93rd year and think I will stop. We are all together and thank the Lord for all His goodness and mercy, His loving guiding in all our ways and in everything. This has been written over some years a little at a time.

So many prayers answered, my children and grandchildren all the Lord's and others I have prayed for, some mentioned in this book. Praise and Glory be unto Him.

The view of the back garden from Alice's bedroom at Chard

AFTERWORD

Alice died of heart failure in Chard Hospital on 4 February 1977. She was 97 and outlived all her younger sisters.

Nellie, as she noted, died at 63. Ruth was in her eighties when she died at Hutton; Fred had died 10 years earlier. Aggie was in her nineties when she died, although she did not reach the age that Alice did.

Nellie's adopted daughter Eva died of cancer in St Christopher's, a hospice near Crystal Palace, in 1976. Len died of pneumonia and hypothermia in 1990, aged 81. Nesta died less than two months later, aged 71, after a series of strokes. Alice's stepsons David and Jim are dead.

Bertha is still living in the bungalow in Chard and writing her own life story. The land in front now has houses on it but the fields remain at the back. Her friend Nellie* developed Alzheimer's disease and had to go into hospital.

Grandson David still lives in Weymouth and is retired. One of his sons is married, the other is at home. Granddaughter Diana and family are also in Weymouth. Two of Diana's three children, a daughter and a son, are married. The unmarried son is at university.

Mrs Tucker is 101 and in a nursing home in Northern Ireland but does not recognise anyone.

* Nellie died in March 1997.

195

Bill of Bulwell
by Bill Cross

This is the story of a Nottingham working man. As a child, Bill watched returned soldiers from the First World War live in poverty. He saw miners turned away from the pits each day after seeking work. He vowed he would never become a soldier or a miner. But he became both.

'Ordinary' Lives ①

Series Editor: Ruth I. Johns

BILL OF BULWELL by Bill Cross is available through bookshops or Libraries. Or it can be ordered direct from Plowright Press, Box 66, Warwick CV34 4XE £6.96 (post free UK)